SURFING CALIFORNIA

The Hollister Ranch . . . 1963.

Mountain & Sea Publishing
P.O. Box 126
Redondo Beach, CA. 90277

(213) 379-9321

LCCN 73-78956   ISBN 0-911449-02-7

I use recycled paper. No trees were cut down to make this paper. It was made from paper out of the trash........Bank Wright

"Take care of the earth and it will take care of you"

Mountain & Sea Book

Foreword

A lot of things that hurt surfing
also hurt California . . .
Inaccessible beaches
Irresponsible development
Crowds.

To help surfing
And save the coast
is a formidable task.
But it's not impossible.

To open new beaches
To control development
And to preserve what is left
won't be easy.
But we must try.

This book won't save beaches
or stop shoreline destruction.
But because of it you just may become
more aware of the environment.

And when you're aware . . .
The battle is half won.

Along the California coast
May 5, 1973
Bank Wright

Contents

INDEX TO NORTHERN CALIFORNIA MAPS

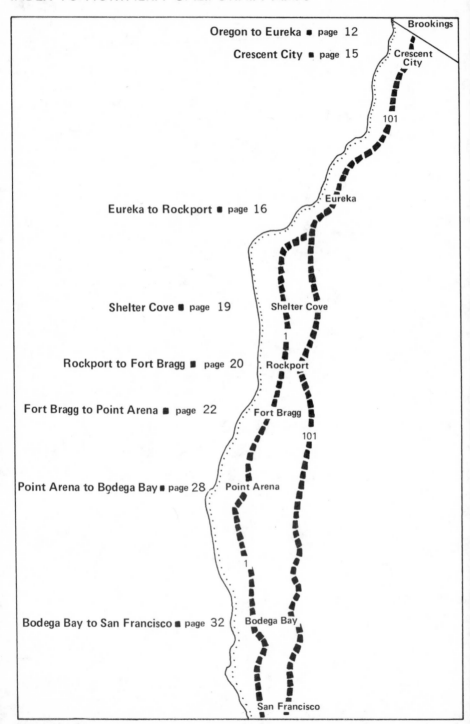

Brookings

Crescent City

101

Eureka

Shelter Cove

1

Rockport

Fort Bragg

101

Point Arena

1

Bodega Bay

San Francisco

INDEX TO CENTRAL CALIFORNIA MAPS

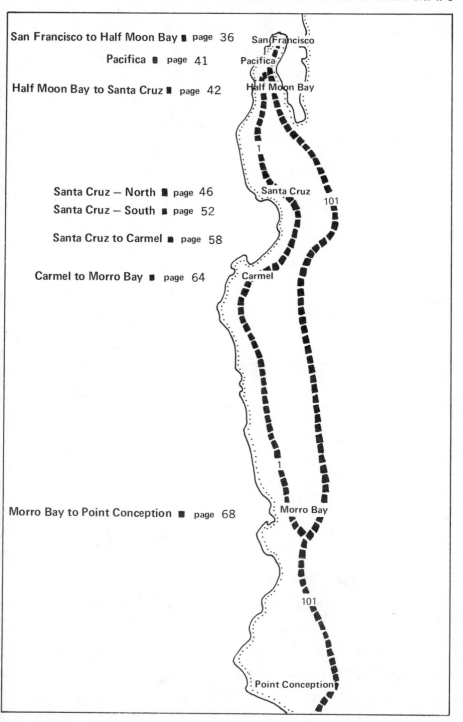

San Francisco

Pacifica

Half Moon Bay

1

Santa Cruz

101

Carmel

1

Morro Bay

101

Point Conception

INDEX TO SOUTHERN CALIFORNIA MAPS

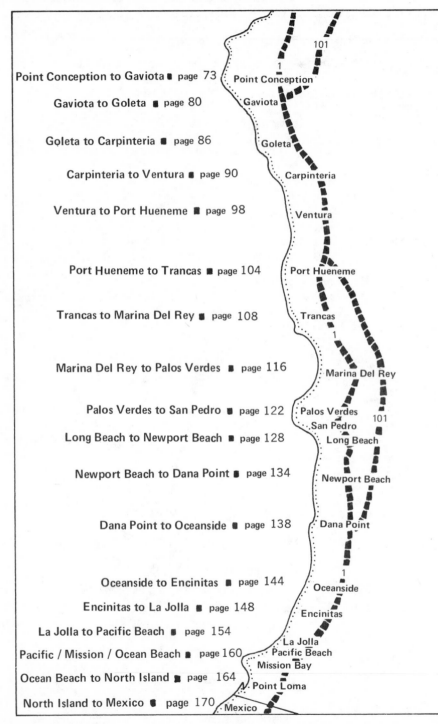

Point Conception
Gaviota
Goleta
Carpinteria
Ventura
Port Hueneme
Trancas
Marina Del Rey
Palos Verdes
San Pedro
Long Beach
Newport Beach
Dana Point
Oceanside
Encinitas
La Jolla
Pacific Beach
Mission Bay
Point Loma
Mexico

101
1

Winter

Spring

Summer

Fall

The seasons are important to surfing. Not only do they tell the kind of weather to expect, they also indicate the type of swell and the months in which to expect it. The following are short descriptions of the four surfing seasons.

FALL (September — November) This is one of the best times to surf. During these months you can ride both summer and winter surf. Late south swells still break in September and October and by the middle of October the first north and west swells begin to show . . . Wave shape is excellent. During summer the sands have had a chance to settle, leaving a contoured bottom over which the first winter swells break with machine-like precision.

WINTER (November — March) These are cold, wet months of the year. Months when the ocean temperature drops noticeably as cold currents flow down from Alaska. Winter surf is big, strong, and consistent . . . it is also unpredictable. Strong winds, currents, and shifting bottom sand makes for erratic and unreliable breaking patterns.

SPRING (March — May) These are months of waiting — waiting for summer surf. Winter swells still break but show a steady decrease in size and frequency. They come and go quickly — lasting only a day or two . . . Then, usually in May, the first signs of summer are felt. South swells once again begin to rumble out of the South Pacific. Summer has started.

SUMMER (May — September) South swells are sporadic through May and most of June. But as summer moves along they steadily increase in size and frequency. A series of 3-6 foot swells can be counted on through September and "freak" summer swells even break in October. In general, summer surf is smaller, less frequent, and not as strong as winter.

Swell Direction

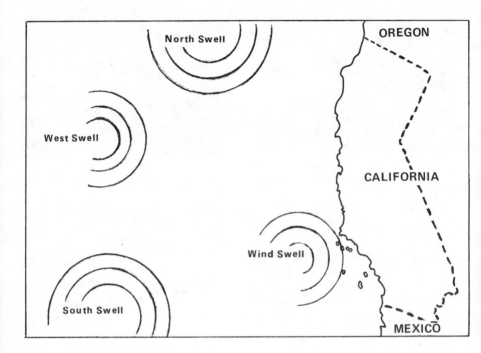

One of the most important elements affecting California surf is the direction from which the swell originates. This geographical position determines which areas will receive the swell and the shape of the surf when it breaks. **FOR EXAMPLE:** Malibu Point breaks perfectly during a south swell, but a north or west swell have no effect ! **ALSO:** A northwest swell will break at almost every spot in Santa Cruz — except for Stockton Avenue which needs a south.

The following types of swells produce surf along the California coast:

NORTH SWELL: A winter swell — generated by storms in the North Pacific. Common from December through February. Average size: 3-6 feet, can reach 10-15. Caution: can carry large amounts of "Aleutian Juice" (power).

WEST SWELL: Originates in the Western Pacific. Common during fall and spring months. Size averages from 3-6 feet. Variations such as a "southwest" or a "northwest" occur as storms move north or south of the equator.

SOUTH SWELL: Born from storms in the South Pacific. Most common between May and September. Average size: 3-6 feet. 8-15 foot swells are not unusual. These swells appear as long, well-defined lines — visible for miles to sea.

WIND SWELL / PEAK SWELL: A "local" swell. Created by a strong wind 100-200 miles from shore. Appear bumpy and irregular but can produce excellent surf. Size ranges from 1-8 feet. Common for 1 or 2 days after a storm or strong wind.

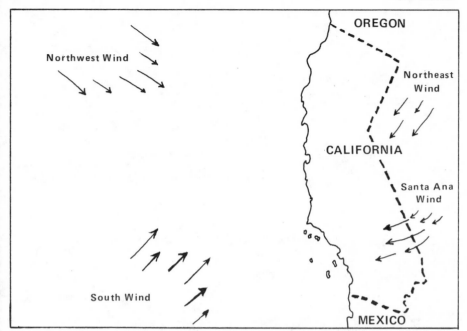

Seawinds have a tremendous effect upon surfing in California. They directly influence both the wave's shape and the ocean's surface condition. Wind can quickly turn smooth well-shaped surf into unridable chop in a matter of minutes. It is important to understand where they come from and the effect they produce.

NORTHWEST WIND: The normal seabreeze. Referred to as "the prevailing wind". Usually starts by late morning and lasts throughout the day. This wind blows "onshore" and destroys the surf. **Note:** Sometimes it dies off as sunset approaches. This produces what is called an "evening glass off". — smooth water that's perfect for surfing.

NORTHEAST WIND: A rare winter wind. Usually follows a rainstorm and lasts only a day or two. It can produce either an "offshore" or "sidewind" effect on the surf — depending upon the geographical location of the surf spot.

SOUTH WIND: An unfavorable breeze from a southerly direction. Its rare, but when it blows the ocean quickly turns to bumpy chop.

SANTA ANA WINDS: A warm, desert wind peculiar to Southern California. Blows "offshore" producing fast, hardbreaking surf. Common during summer but can occur anytime.

These winds produce the following effects upon the surf:

ONSHORE: Unfavorable. Blows "onto" the land and quickly destroys any semblance of smooth water.

OFFSHORE: A beneficial wind. Blows "off" the land and directly into the oncoming surf. Not only does it smooth the water but it momentarily holds the crest allowing the surfer time to slip beneath.

SIDEWIND: A favorable wind if it's not too strong. Blows parallel to the shore and produces conditions similar to an offshore. Common a day or two after a winter storm.

"The Fairgrounds" -- VENTURA POINT. Between medium and low tide the waves get fast and tubular. Sometimes they're makeable, sometimes not. Today it's perfect and the locals are ripping.

SUPER TUBES works best at low tide. At high tide, the surf breaks on the rocks.

LA JOLLA SHORES — The tide is high and the waves are thick and easybreaking.

The natural movement of the tides has an important effect upon surfing. It determines both when and where you surf and the shape of the waves once you get there.

Depending on the size of the swell, many areas will be ridable at one tide but not another. For example, some reefs are unridable at low tide due to exposed rocks and holes. These same reefs are safe at any other tide. Or spots located in front of cliffs may be unsurfable at high tide due to waves rebounding off the rocks.

The tide also affects the shape of the surf. At lower tides waves tend to break top-to-bottom leaving very little room for manuevering. As the volume of water increases (incoming high tide), the waves become thicker with larger areas on increases (incoming high tide), the surf becomes thicker with large areas on which to surf.

Remember, these are general statements. Each spot is different. Only by actually experiencing the tide change will you learn the characteristics of that particular area.

THE AREA: This section of the book covers from the coastal town of Brookings, Oregon to the mouth of San Francisco Bay.

THE LAND: Natural is the best way to describe the coast of Northern California. Little has changed since the first settlers arrived. Towns have arisen, small industry has been built, but in general the land is unscarred.
Rolling ranchlands slope gently into the sea, sandy beaches that few humans have ever seen, rivers that flow freely to the sea — this is the land of the north coast. The surfing potential is unlimited. The spots mentioned are only a few. Hundreds of new breaks await discovery.

THE PEOPLE: Like the land, the people are mellow. They are not concerned with the hassles of city living. Theirs is a simple life — close to the land. When you depend on the earth for your living you learn to respect it and take care of it. Surfers traveling north should try and leave their city habits at home. This way they'll better understand and enjoy the beauty of the north coast.

ACCESSIBILITY: A large portion of this rugged north coast is inaccessible. Private ranches, sub divisions, and sheer cliffs restrict direct public access . . . Most of the surf spots can be easily reached from either Hwy 1 or Hwy 101. When a break is located in front of private property it will be stated so in the text and possible entry routes suggested. **Note:** Most land owners will allow surfers to cross their property if they first "ask permission" and then treat the land as if it were their own.

WEATHER: The further north you go the cooler it gets. Winter months are cold and rainy with long stretches when surfing is impossible. It's "hit or miss" If you're lucky you'll catch 2 or 3 consecutive days of good weather . . . Summer is a little better. The sun comes out and warms up the land. Surfing improves but watch out for the fog. When it rolls in everything comes to a stop — including surfing.

WATER TEMPERATURE: The water is cold — very cold. Temperatures range from 43 degrees to 55 degrees year'-round. Full wetsuits are a must. Boots and gloves are recommended. Remember . . . it's super cold, so be prepared.

TIDE: The tide is very important to surfing in Northern California. Many of the spots are reef breaks and the tide level will determine if it's safe or too dangerous to surf. Refer to the tide suggested in the text.

CAMPING: Beach parks dot the shoreline from San Francisco to Oregon. Some allow camping, some don't. Weekdays the parks are usually empty — weekends they're full. Due to heavy summer crowds, advance reservations are sometimes necessary . . . An "off season" camping book is available at a reduced rate. Ask a park ranger for information. **Note:** If you become drowsy and are far from a campground, the Highway Patrol recommends pulling off the road. Hwy 1 is extremely dangerous — especially if you're tired. The following parks allow camping:

> Patrick's Point State Park
> Mac Kerricher State Park
> Russian Gulch State Park
> Van Damme State Park
> Manchester State Park
> Salt Point State Park
> Sonoma Coast State Park

NORTHERN CALIFORNIA

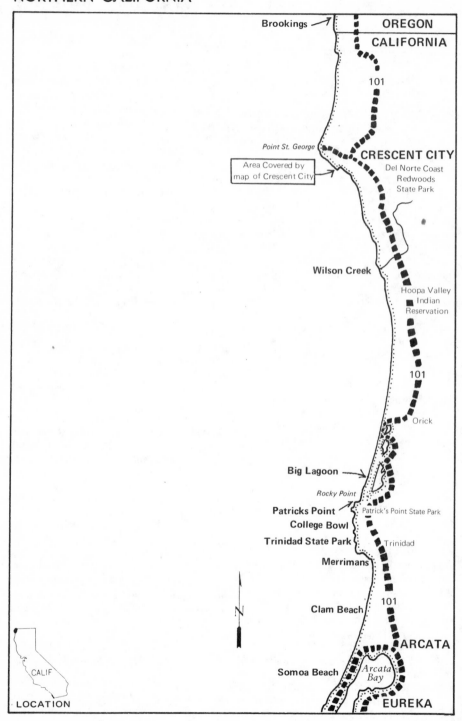

Brookings

OREGON

CALIFORNIA

101

Point St. George

CRESCENT CITY

Area Covered by
map of Crescent City

Del Norte Coast
Redwoods
State Park

Wilson Creek

Hoopa Valley
Indian
Reservation

101

Orick

Big Lagoon

Rocky Point

Patricks Point

Patrick's Point State Park

College Bowl

Trinidad State Park

Trinidad

Merrimans

N

Clam Beach

101

ARCATA

Somoa Beach

Arcata
Bay

EUREKA

CALIF

LOCATION

BROOKINGS, OREGON — The first surfable spot north of the California/Oregon border. Large surf breaks with the same shape as pictured above.

A winter line peels across an outer sandbar — BIG LAGOON.

The lineup at PATRICKS POINT. Ride ends in channel to right of photo.

Brookings

A small seaside village 20 miles north of Crescent City. Long peeling lines off a central peak. Breaks ⅛ mile out. Waves are soft and easy breaking. Fast and tubular across an inside reef. Takes any winter swell, 2-8 feet. Medium low tide. Sandy beach. Camping allowed in nearby park. **Comment:** A small taste of what the rest of Oregon is like!

Wilson Creek

A rugged, rarely ridden creek break . . . a few miles south of Crescent City. Isolated and a long way from help. Requires side trip off Hwy 101.

Big Lagoon

Explosive winter walls! Breaks outside a sandy peninsula. Size is deceptive . . . can look 5 and be 10. Isn't surfed much . . . too big and lonely.

Patrick's Point

A rocky point break north of Eureka. Two separate peaks: a long (sometimes hollow) left ½ way to point and a thick, hardbreaking beach peak. Both need a 3-8 foot west swell. Medium tide. **Note:** Camping allowed in state park. **Caution:** Dangerous shorebreak along nearby Agate Beach.

College Bowl

A small wave beach break. Shifting peak. Works on a 2-4 foot south or west swell. Medium low tide. Sandy bottom - shape is unpredictable. 1½ miles north of Trinidad Head . . . off Hwy 101.

Trinidad State Park

Strong, shifting peaks exploding over jagged reefs. Very temperamental. Ridable at medium high tide only! From park take narrow dirt trail that descends to beach. Always worth a look.

NORTHERN CALIFORNIA

Slow winter lines peel across BROOKING'S Reef.

Early morning swells roll into BIG LAGOON.

TRINIDAD STATE PARK — Strong currents and lots of rocks.

A taste of Oregon. Hundreds of spots like this await discovery.

Clam and Somoa Beach

Winter: Massive walls everywhere. Peaks are well-shaped but getting out is impossible. Endless soup lines. Normal channels closed out . . . a dangerous place to surf.

Summer: Small south swells produce clean beach peaks along 4 miles of sandy, uncrowded beach. Channels for easy access. A safe time to swim or surf.

Merriman's

Long lines breaking across outer sand-bars. Mostly rights, some lefts. Winter waves are big . . . getting out difficult. Summer months are calmer - a safer time to surf.

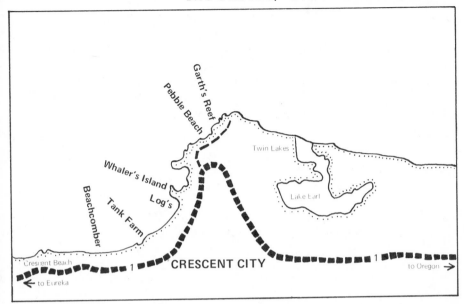

CRESCENT CITY
The last California town before entering the state of Oregon. Has good surf and cold water all year. Following are the popular surfing areas:

Garth's Reef
A right point break . . . north of town. Outer reef produces a thick, soupy wall that reforms and breaks again over a shallow rock shelf. Works on any swell. Needs low tide. Best in winter. Private land - but access is not restricted.

Pebble Beach
Two way beach peaks. Soft takeoffs with fast, thin tubes. Takes any swell, 2-6 feet. Medium low tide. Rock and clay bottom. Peaks feather at high tide. **Caution:** Watch for floating logs at high tide!

Whaler's Island
A thin right wall. Peaks near island and peels over a shallow ledge. Needs strong winter swell, 3-8 feet. Ridden when all else is closed out. Best at low tide. **Caution:** Watch for exposed rocks near takeoff.

Logs
Beach peaks next to jetty. Needs a 1-5 foot south swell. Sand bottom and beach. Best in summer, has small winter surf too.

Tank Farm
Peaks with right and left lines. Takes any swell. Breaks from 1-5 feet, medium high tide. Located across from kerosene tanks on Hwy 101.

Beachcomber
A mile of shifting beach peaks. Breaks on any swell from 1-5 feet. Sandy beach and bottom. Main peak located in front of Beachcomber restaurant. A year'-round spot.

Cold lines peel onto CRESCENT BEACH.

15

NORTHERN CALIFORNIA

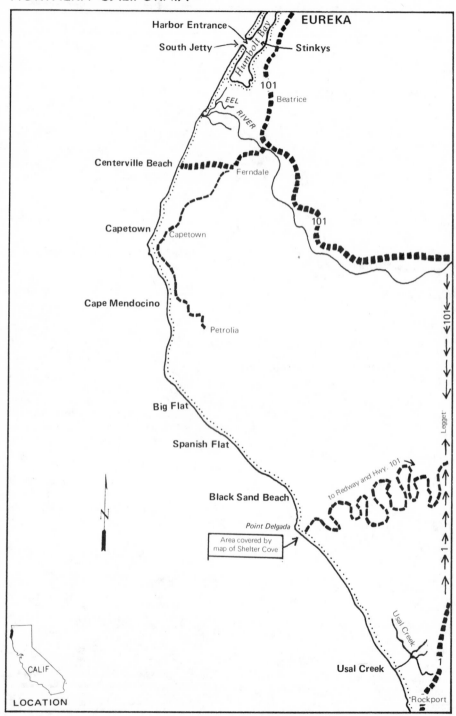

EUREKA

Harbor Entrance
South Jetty
Stinkys
Humbolt Bay
101
Beatrice
EEL RIVER
Centerville Beach
Ferndale
Capetown
Capetown
101
Cape Mendocino
Petrolia
Big Flat
Spanish Flat
101 Leggett
to Redway and Hwy. 101
Black Sand Beach
Point Delgada
Area covered by
map of Shelter Cove
N
1
Usal Creek
Usal Creek
Rockport

CALIF

LOCATION

STINKY'S — A mile inside Humboldt Bay. Swells have rolled down entrance channel (background), wrapped left, and are peeling across a winter sandbar.

HARBOR ENTRANCE — Pictured above is an unusual phenomenon. A large winter swell has rolled down the entrance to Humboldt Bay and is breaking inside the main channel.

Harbor Entrance
A spooky winter spot. Breaks along inside edge of north seawall. Long, tubular lefts peel across deep sandbars. Needs a 5-10 foot swell and medium-low tide. **Caution:** Massive currents run in and out of bay . . . use extreme caution at all times.

Stinky's
Big winter ground swells roll down entrance channel and break inside Humboldt Bay (2 miles from ocean). Needs a 6-15 foot swell and low tide. Sandbar peaks with long, slow rights and lefts. Always smooth. Private property hinders access.

South Jetty
South swells rebound off rocks and form fast, well-shaped peaks. Needs a 2-6 swell and medium tide. Winter waves are usually too big and unpredictable. A sandy beach with piles of driftwood. Reached by dirt road along south peninsula. A good summer spot.

Centerville Beach
A rarely (if ever) surfed beach break . . . a few country miles off Hwy 101. Hard-breaking peaks and lines - ¼ mile offshore. Breaks on any swell from 1-5 feet. Medium tide. **Caution:** Strong rip currents and a long ways from help.

NORTHERN CALIFORNIA

Capetown

A series of reefs extending a mile to sea. Numerous peaks in front of private ranchland. Takes any swell from 3-20 feet. As surf grows - peaks keep moving further out. Frequent clean-up sets and strong currents. Easily blown out by northwest winds. **Comment:** Like the Tijuana Sloughs . . . lots of potential with the right conditions.

Cape Mendocino

Miles and miles of unridden reef and beach breaks. Similar to Point Conception . . . private ranchland with countless points and bays. Winter surf is big and consistent. Weather is cold and unpredictable. Breaks year'round . . . any swell-any tide. **Comment:** An untapped supply of surf.

Big Flat and Spanish Flat

Private ranchlands along a remote section of California coast. Reports say . . . "Winter waves too big and consistent but summer swells are "hot n glassy". Dirt roads lead in but permission from owners must be obtained. Plans call for a new Hwy along this section of coastline.

Black Sand Beach

An isolated sandy beach. Offshore reefs produce peeling lines along northern stretch of coast (see map). Winter surf is big and unpredictable. Best in summer when 2-5 foot souths pour onto the reefs. Requires a long hike or sand buggy ride from Shelter Cove. **Comment:** Viewed through binoculars - looks like Lower Trestles.

Usal Creek

An isolated break north of Rockport. Breaks all year from 2-8 feet. Medium tide. Shape is unpredictable. Reached by destructive dirt road off Hwy 1 (see map).

Turning back at SHELTER COVE.

The "second reef" — SHELTER COVE.

WIDOW'S PEAK — This gnarly looking peak breaks in only 3-4 feet of water. Shelter Cove locals consider it their answer to the "Bonzai Pipeline".

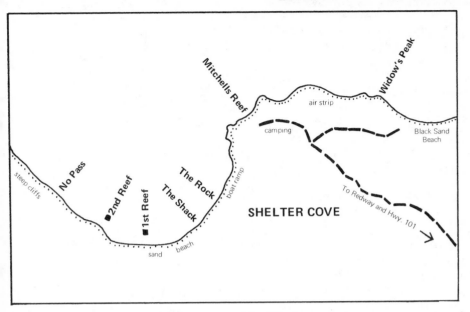

SHELTER COVE

A private coastal development far removed from the speed of city life. Breaks year'round. Winter surf is big and cold . . . summer waves are small but well-shaped. **Note:** Size is deceptive when viewing from bluffs. Usually 2 or 3 feet bigger! The surf breaks are as follows:

Widow's Peak

A gnarly left. Peaks off a rocky point and spits shoreward. Breaks on any winter swell from 5-15 feet. Hardly ever ridden. **Comment:** Pipeline and Wedge rolled into one!

Mitchell's Reef

A big wave break just north of main cove. Works on the biggest of winter swells. Close-out sets and rocks . . . a big drawback. Rarely ridden.

The Rock

A soft, easy left slide. Breaks on any 1-5 foot swell. Medium-low tide. Just south of boat ramp. **Caution:** Watch for submerged rock in lineup.

The Shack

A soft peak with an easy right or left slide. Breaks from 2-6 feet - any swell. Medium tide best. A strong south swell gives it kick. Prevailing winds blow offshore. **Comment:** A touchy surf spot . . . a "hit or miss" situation.

First Reef

An offshore reef. Feathering curls both right and left. Grinds and spits as it nears shore. Ends in crushing shorebreak. Breaks on any swell from 2-5 feet. Medium-low tide. **Comment:** Its got juice.

Second Reef

Swells peak over a triangular bed of rocks and peel into deep water. Best in winter on a 2-8 foot swell. Medium tide. First and Second reefs connect on bigger swells. Located in front of fresh water stream - south end of cove. **Comment:** The class wave of Shelter Cove.

No Pass

A big, tubular left. Breaks over a jagged reef onto a sandy beach. Needs a 2-10 foot winter swell. Medium-low tide. Last ridable spot of cove. **Comment:** A real pump and grinder.

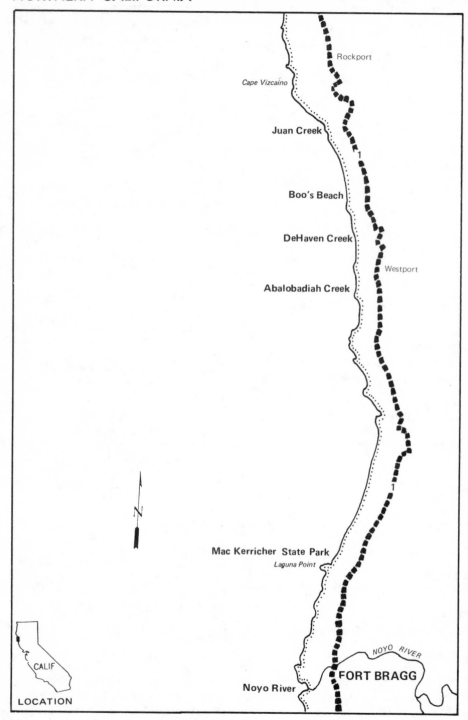

Rockport

Cape Vizcaíno

Juan Creek

1

Boo's Beach

DeHaven Creek

Westport

Abalobadiah Creek

1

Mac Kerricher State Park

Laguna Point

NOYO RIVER

FORT BRAGG

Noyo River

CALIF

LOCATION

Juan Creek

Thick walls that peak on an outside reef. Breaks on any winter swell from 2-8 feet. Medium tide. **Caution:** Huge rocks along shoreline. **Note:** Last ridable spot before Hwy 1 turns inland.

Boo's Beach

Perfect right lines off a small reef. Best on 2-6 foot winter swells. Very rocky inside . . . must have medium-high tide. 1 mile north of Westport. **Comment:** A super tube but very temperamental.

De Haven Creek

2 way peaks over a rocky creek bed. Works on any swell. Closes out above 5 feet. Rarely surfed . . . shape is too unreliable. Best bet is during summer months.

MacKerricher State Park

Small 2 way peaks. Breaks in front of park's main beach. Takes a winter swell from 1-5 feet. Medium-low tide. A spot for the locals of Fort Bragg. Camping facilities available.

Abalobadiah Creek

Small right and left peaks. Best on a 1-5 foot south swell. Winter surf is big and gnarly. A summer spot. Marked by a colorful farm house along Hwy 1.

Noyo River

A slow-poke left off north seawall of harbor entrance. Needs a large winter swell and low tide. Temperamental and unreliable. Just off Hwy 1 on way into Fort Bragg.

Feathering lines of JUAN CREEK.

Medium tide at BOO'S BEACH.

A small wave rolls along the Noyo Harbor seawall. It needs a big swell and low tide before it works.

BOO'S BEACH is a very tempermental reef break. When it's working it can't be beat. But as the tide drops, sections appear in the lineup. At low tide the reef closes out.

21

NORTHERN CALIFORNIA

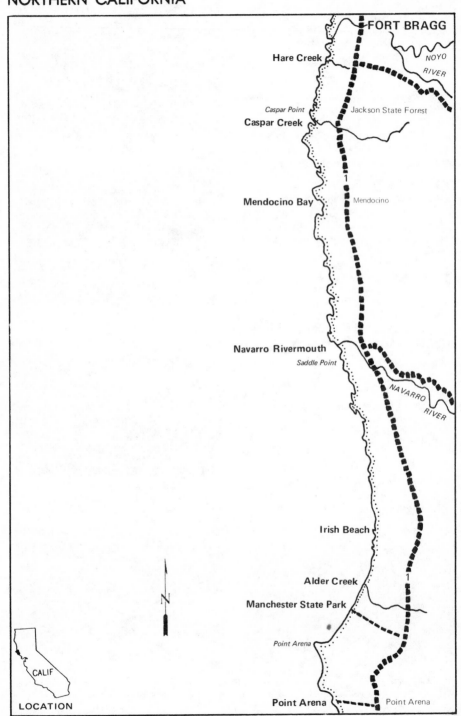

Hare Creek

Smooth, soft beach waves. At one time the main break of Fort Bragg. Now . . . rarely ridden. Takes any swell from 1-5 feet. Medium-low tide. **Comment:** Shape is very unreliable.

Caspar Creek

A good learning spot. Small (1-3 foot) sliders in a protected cove (photo). Best after a rain when creeks deposit fresh sand. Off Hwy 1 before the little village of Caspar. A safe place to surf.

Small lines at CASPAR CREEK.

MENDOCINO BAY

A large, deep water bay. Just south of village. Thick ground swells move into bay and generate surf in 3 spots:

The Beach: A beach and point break. Shifting peaks and lines. Bumpy and restless in winter. Best in summer when bottom settles and south swells roll.

The Reef: A big wave break off south point. High powered walls that blast across a shallow reef. Needs a 10-20 foot winter swell. Medium-low tide. A steep takeoff and thick shoulder. **Comment:** Breaks like Waimea Bay (Hawaii).

"The beach" — MENDOCINO BAY.

SMUGGLER'S COVE — trying to break.

A 10 foot winter line explodes off the beach at NAVARRO RIVERMOUTH. River is in foreground.

Small farms dot the coastline from San Francisco to Rockport.

NORTHERN CALIFORNIA

Smuggler's Cove
A protected cove - south end of bay. Thick, easy peaks with flat, powerless shoulders. Takes a winter swell from 6-15 feet. Medium-low tide. **Note:** Area is private . . . access is difficult.

Navarro Rivermouth
Hardbreaking sandbar peaks. Needs a 2-8 foot winter swell. Medium tide. Shape depends on sand flow from river. **Caution:** Sewage at rivermouth attracts many large sharks!

Irish Beach
A small woodsy beach north of Irish Cove. Takes any swell from 2-8 feet. Medium tide. Area has 3 different breaks . . . An easy right slide off the north point. Ends atop a pile of rocks . . . A machine-like left peak in the middle of beach (photo). Also, a suckular left off the south point. Usually bumpy and rarely ridden. **Comment:** All good waves but the left in the middle is best.

Alder Creek
A potent winter break. Sandbar peaks on both sides of creek. Fast drops with thick, tubular walls. Starts to cook on 2-8 foot swells. Medium-low tide. Summer waves are soft and mellow. North of Manchester. Take side road off Hwy 1.

Manchester State Park
Steep winter walls . . . big and dangerous. Ridable from 1-5 feet, medium tide. A strong beach break. Best in summer when swells are small. Overnight camping allowed.

A small line peels off the north point of IRISH BEACH. Wave ends quickly on a shallow reef (whitewater in foreground).

"Middle's" — IRISH BEACH. Easy lefts that few have ever surfed!

POINT ARENA — Winter lines smoke onto "the point" reef. Paddling channel runs parallel to pier. Exposed reef (extreme right) awaits lost boards.

ALDER CREEK is a remote and rarely surfed beach break a few miles north of Point Arena. It consists of a series of sandbars with peaks and lines that break in front of a rugged, black sand beach. The top photo shows the north sandbar. The bottom shows another sandbar located south of the creek. **Note:** Structure (left of photos) is not a lifeguard tower. It's an outhouse provided by the local farmers.

POINT ARENA is like what Southern California was back in 1940. No crowds, only a few cars, and lots of room. It's a small coastal village that is yet unscarred by human progress . . . It also has good surf. Pictured above is an average winter's day. Long west lines stack to the horizon. And note: nobody out!

NORTHERN CALIFORNIA

An average day at "The Channel" reef of Point Arena. The surf is 2-3 feet with sets of 5 and 6. Tide is medium-high. The lefts are working better than the rights but both are makeable. For a better view of the lineup see photo at bottom of next page.

Famous Hwy 1 — a real twister!

A lonely hook at POINT ARENA.

Many who live along the north coast have their own private surfing spots.

The "north point" of Mendocino Bay. As yet unridden.

POINT ARENA

A small, mellow town along Hwy 1 having two nice breaks near old fishing pier.

The Point: A concentrated peak. Steep, hooking takeoff followed by a thick right shoulder. Spits across inside reef. Kelp bulbs mark the paddling channel. Needs a 2-10 foot winter swell, medium-high tide. **Caution:** Razor sharp inside reef leashes a must!

The Channel: A peak left, south of old pier. Breaks 2-10 feet on winter swells. Medium tide. Lines peel next to deep channel. Exposed rocks. **Comment:** Like Ala Moana . . . but not as tubular.

Looking north from Point Arena . . . In the center of photo is small winter surf breaking across "The Point" reef. The finger of land (extreme right) is Point Arena. **Note:** During big swells, thick lines can be seen peeling off this point but it is as yet untried.

Different views of "The Channel" at Point Arena.

"The Channel" surf of Point Arena.

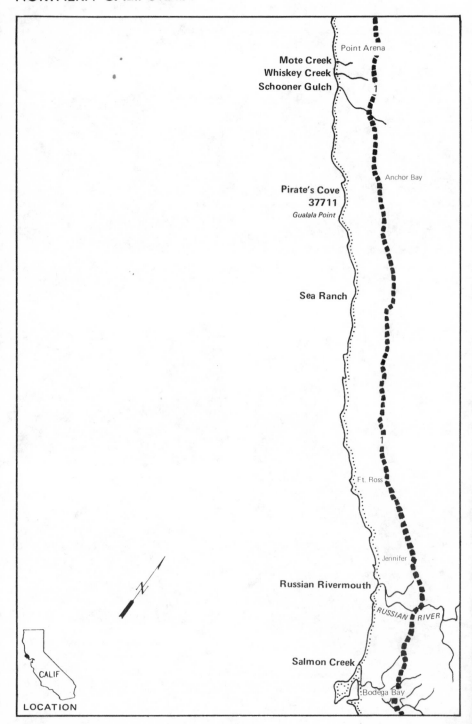

Point Arena

Mote Creek
Whiskey Creek
Schooner Gulch

1

Anchor Bay

Pirate's Cove
37711
Gualala Point

Sea Ranch

1

Ft. Ross

Jennifer

Russian Rivermouth

RUSSIAN RIVER

Salmon Creek

Bodega Bay

N

CALIF

LOCATION

Mote Creek

A seldom surfed peak break a few miles south of Point Arena. Shifting peaks off a small reef ⅛ mile below creek. Takes any swell, 2-8 feet. Medium tide. Land is private . . . but owner doesn't mind visitors. Watch for creek marker along Hwy.

Whiskey Creek

Long rights off point. Usually mushy and sectiony. Breaks from 2-8 feet - summer and winter. Medium-low tide. Usually good in the late evenings. A temperamental break. First creek south of Mote.

Schooner Gulch

A reef and beach break. Peak lefts that peel toward creek. Blows out early. Breaks on most swells from 2-6 feet. Medium tide. Best on evening glass offs. Soft, easy waves. Good for beginners.

Pirates Cove

A secluded, sheltered cove. Shifty lefts over a sandy bottom. Takes any winter swell up to 5 feet. Medium-low tide. Usually glassy. - except on south winds. **Comment:** A safe place with consistent surf.

SCHOONER GULCH — With the right conditions, rides from in front of the trees to the small creek are possible.

The pop-up peaks of WHISKEY CREEK.

The small rights of 37711.

Delicate lines at SEA RANCH. Note: Marine grass (foreground) is rare to California's coast.

NORTHERN CALIFORNIA

PIRATES COVE — A small but well-shaped line peels across the cove. For some reason, this spot is rarely surfed.

The economy of Northern California is built upon the logging industry. Pictured is a scene typical of the early morning . . . A fully loaded logg'n truck heads for the mill, while outside an empty comber heads for shore.

37711
A clean, easy right line. Breaks from 1-5 feet · any winter swell. Medium-low tide. Large surf is unridable. Across from red house at 37711 Hwy 1.
Caution: Watch for surface rocks near end of wave.

Sea Ranch
Miles of unexplored points and bays · unlimited potential. Coastline is being subdivided and turned into a private residential development. Shoreline is rocky with many virgin beaches. Breaks on any swell · with ridable surf year-round. No local surfers. Area is rarely ridden. See photo for glimpse of potential !

ENJOY - DON'T DESTROY
AREA BELOW BLUFFS FOR NEXT 1000 FEET SOUTH IS A MARINE PRESERVE. NO COLLECTING OF MARINE LIFE - INCLUDING ABALONE - PLEASE! T.S.R.A.

SEA RANCH — smooth and fragile

Lines of the RUSSIAN RIVERMOUTH.

The peaks of the Russian River.

SALMON CREEK — One of the most consistent, well-shaped beach breaks north of San Francisco. Note: Not shown here are the strong rip-currents and sharks that make surfing a bit risky.

North coast beaches can produce fantastic surf under the right conditions. WRIGHT'S BEACH is just one of them.

Russian Rivermouth

Long (sometimes tubular) right lines. Shape depends on contour of shifting sand bottom. Very unpredictable. Best in winter on a 2-8 foot swell. Medium-low tide. **Caution:** Scavenger sharks feed at river's end.

Salmon Creek

A wide, sandy beach break. Takes any swell and will hold shape from 2-12 feet. Medium tide. Winter surf is usually big and powerful - getting outside difficult. Best in summer on small (2-5 foot) south swells. **Caution:** Strong rip currents and sharks.

NORTHERN CALIFORNIA

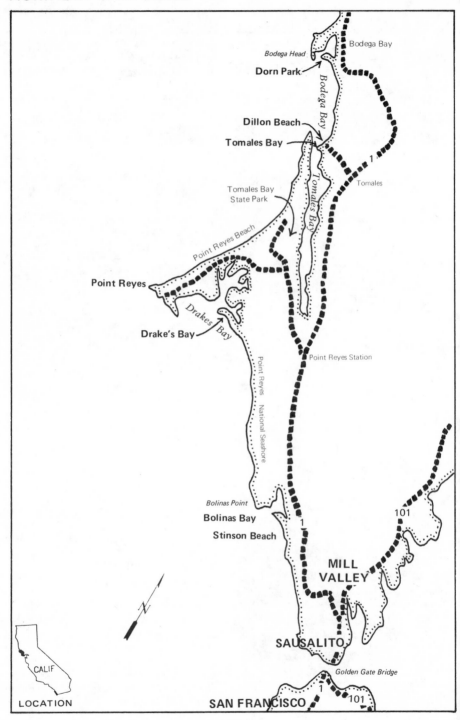

Bodega Bay

Bodega Head

Dorn Park

Bodega Bay

Dillon Beach

Tomales Bay

7

Tomales

Tomales Bay
State Park

Tomales Bay

Point Reyes Beach

Point Reyes

Drakes Bay

Drake's Bay

Point Reyes National Seashore

Point Reyes Station

Bolinas Point

101

Bolinas Bay

Stinson Beach

1

**MILL
VALLEY**

SAUSALITO

Golden Gate Bridge

1

SAN FRANCISCO

101

CALIF

LOCATION

32

Dorn Park
Unpredictable beach peaks. Usually just shorebreak. Sandy beach and bottom. A county park . . . no camping.

Dillon Beach
A secluded beach break . . . 10 miles off Hwy 1 (see map). Long, point-like lines. Breaks from 2-10 feet, any swell (winter best), medium-low tide. **Comment:** Well worth the side trip if all conditions are right.

Tomales Bay
Sandbar peaks at foot of bay entrance (see map). Clean, (sometimes long) rights and lefts. Takes any winter swell. Best from 2-6 feet, medium-low tide. **Note:** An isolated break - many miles off the beaten path. Good waves but rarely ridden.

Point Reyes
Massive winter peaks off tip of point. Reports of 20-60 foot walls. As yet unridden . . . and likely to remain so. **Comment:** California's answer to Kaena Point (Hawaii).

Drake's Bay
A long stretch of white sand beach. Located inside Point Reyes National Forest Reserve. Breaks on all swells but south is best. Shape is very unreliable. Even without surf the natural beauty of park is worth the trip. Camping allowed - see ranger for information.

Bolinas Bay
Winter sandbars produce small, point-like tubes on both sides of bay entrance. Breaks on most swells - from 2-4 feet, medium-low tide. **Caution:** Signs in Bolinas warn against swimming . . . waters are polluted!!

Stinson Beach
A mellow beach town, 20 twisting miles north of San Francisco. Miles of uncrowded, rarely surfed, beach peaks. Best in winter a day or two after storm. Ridable from 2-6 feet. Closes out on big swells. Shape changes daily . . . depends on contour of sandy bottom. State park provides access.

Well-defined north swells pour onto deserted DILLON BEACH.

A STINSON BEACH lip.

Small lines at STINSON'S.

POINT REYES BEACH — Although never ridden, this beach can produce some of the most powerful, well-shaped surf in all of California.

A "secret reef" a few miles north of STINSON BEACH.

Unhealthy shooters at BOLINAS BAY.

A northern peak — awaiting discovery.

THE AREA: This section covers the coastline from the entrance of San Francisco Bay to the northern tip of Point Conception. For a more detailed map see page 5.

THE LAND: Most of the central coastline is still in its natural state. Man has not yet worked his concrete magic but there are signs he is trying. Located between the small coastal villages is the real land of California. Rolling green hills that slope gentle into the sea. Sheer rock cliffs — the trademark of Big Sur. And miles of virgin beaches that few humans have ever set foot on. All this and much more is the land of the central coast.

THE PEOPLE: Progress is on the move. San Francisco is pushing south, Los Angeles is working north. People are moving to central coast. The once small villages of Santa Cruz, Monterey, Carmel, and Morro Bay are growing . . . slowly but surely. Surfing is also on the move. More people mean more surfers and more surfers mean bigger crowds. Where will it end? . . . Your guess is as good as any.

ACCESSIBILITY: Huge sections of this coastline are privately owned. Cattle ranches, military bases, and private homes restrict access to hundreds of miles of unexplored shoreline. The most prominent of these areas are Big Sur and Vandenberg A.F.B. It's these areas that will someday reveal hundreds of new spots. But until then they will remain known only to an adventuresome few.

WATER TEMPERATURE: The further north you go the colder it gets. Water temperatures range from 47 degrees to 55 degrees. Full wetsuits are mandatory. Boots and gloves aren't' required but help. During summer you can surf without a wetsuit but you won't last long. The water is cold — all year.

THE TIDE: The tide plays an important role in surfing along the central coast. It can determine whether a beach break is ridable or if a reef is safe. There are no standards — each spot has its own rules. Refer to the text for the "suggested" tide. But remember . . . tide levels vary. A high tide in June may not be the same as a high tide in July. Keep a tidebook handy and seek advice from a local.

CAMPING: The state of California operates a number of beach parks where overnight camping is permitted. Ask any park ranger for the map that lists these parks and their facilities. Also inquire about the special "off season" rate available during winter months. But remember . . . the parks are spaced widely apart. Should you be caught "between" parks, the Highway Patrol would rather see you parked along the road than at the bottom of a cliff. The following parks allow camping:

> Butano State Park
> New Brighton State Beach
> Sunset State Beach
> Pfeiffer Big Sur State Park
> San Simeon State Beach
> Atascadero State Beach
> Morro Bay State Park
> Montana de Oro State Park
> Pismo State Beach
> Jalama County Park

CENTRAL CALIFORNIA

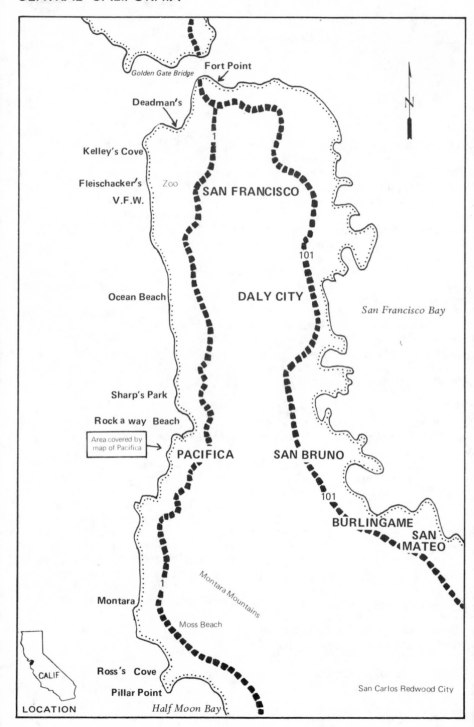

Golden Gate Bridge

Fort Point

Deadman's

Kelley's Cove

Fleischacker's
V.F.W.

Zoo

SAN FRANCISCO

1

101

Ocean Beach

DALY CITY

San Francisco Bay

Sharp's Park

Rock a way Beach

Area covered by
map of Pacifica

PACIFICA

SAN BRUNO

101

BURLINGAME

SAN
MATEO

1

Montara Mountains

Montara

Moss Beach

Ross's Cove

Pillar Point

Half Moon Bay

San Carlos Redwood City

CALIF

LOCATION

Fort Point

Point lefts in front of old fort. A winter spot. Best from 2-6 feet, low tide. Breaks beneath the Golden Gate Bridge. Usually glassy. Rocky shoreline. **Caution:** Strong currents run in and out of bay . . . be careful. Local military authority discourages surfing.

Deadman's

A steep, narrow trail leads along cliffs to a left point break. Thick lines peel into a protected cove. Cooks on 2-10 foot winter swells, medium tide. Rocks . . . use a leash. **Note:** A slip on trail and it's all over.

Kelly's Cove

Perfect beach peaks. Breaks on any swell, 2-15 feet. Medium tide. Big and sometimes too strong during winter. Tubes spit when offshores blow out of City.

Fleischacker's

A gnarly beach peak in front of zoo. Steep and tubular. Takes any swell, 3-10 feet. Medium tide. Best shape is in late spring. **Caution:** Strong downcoast currents during big swells.

V. F. W.

A consistent peak in front of Veterans of Foreign Wars building. Spits and chews on any swell from 2-12 feet. Medium tide. Big and strong in winter. Small and safe in summer.

Ocean Beach

Three miles of beach peaks. Steep and super strong in winter. Breaks all year, 2-12 feet. Medium tide best. Rarely

The lefts of FORT POINT.

The lineup at DEADMAN'S.

A winter day at DEADMAN'S.

KELLEY'S COVE — During heavy surf takeoff point is near last visible line. **Note:** Pipeline (left) is no longer standing.

CENTRAL CALIFORNIA

1962 . . . An "oldie but goodie" of KELLEY'S COVE. In near background is guano-laden "Seal Rock". In far background are the headlands of Marin County. To the right, but out of photo, is the entrance to San Francisco Bay.

Big winter peaks breaking off FLEISCHACKER ZOO.

During heavy surf, most of the beach breaks in California are unridable. Pictured above is SHARP'S PARK on the biggest winter swell of 1972. It's at least 12 feet and still growing.

surfed by locals. **Note:** Dangerous currents during winter months . . . use extreme caution!

Sharp's Park

Two-way peaks along 2 miles of sandy beach. Best on small, 2-6 foot swells. Medium-low tide. Bigger surf closes out. Ridable all year.

Rockaway Beach

Thick, hooking peaks that pump and grind across outer reefs. Takes any swell. Starts to cook from 8-12 feet. Medium-low tide. Access channel on south end of cove. **Note:** A strong big wave break . . . for experienced riders only!

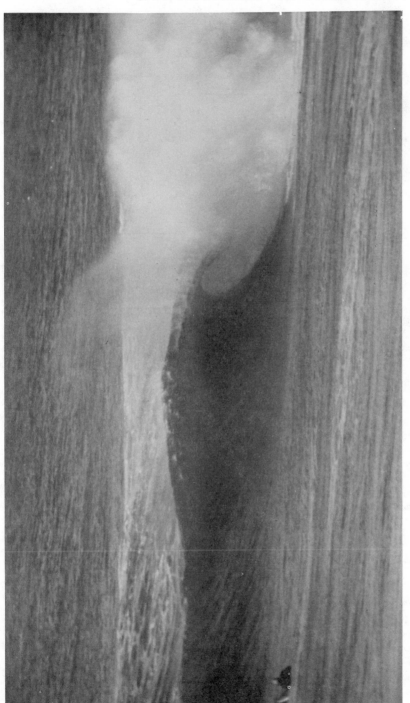

ROCKAWAY BEACH — Located only a few miles below San Francisco, Rockaway can generate some of the strongest winter surf in all of Central California. This is a photo of the "middle peak" during a strong northwest swell and medium-low tide. Note: The "north corner" and the "south corner" can also produce surf like this!

CENTRAL CALIFORNIA

A ROCKAWAY local casually strokes outside while to his right perfect tubes smoke off the "center peak".

December 8, 1964 . . . WANDER'S INN. Dick Keating grabs a rail and goes for it.

Shelter Cove
A small peak left inside cove. Short and fast. Needs a 1-4 foot winter swell, medium tide. Bigger waves close out. A private beach.

Montara
Small, pop-up beach peaks. Surfed on 1-3 foot swells. Unridable on anything bigger. Medium-low tide. Sand beach and bottom. **Comment:** A "sometimes" beach . . . for the Montara locals.

Winter walls off PEDRO POINT.

Ross's Cove
Big, muscular lefts along north side of Pillar Point. Breaks only on the biggest of winter swells. Any tide. Massive currents and rocks add to the danger.
Comment: A gnarly tube that's hardly ever ridden.

Pillar Point
Huge winter walls outside Half Moon Bay harbor. Feather and peel across shallow reefs, almost a mile offshore. Too dangerous for surfing . . . a nice spot to watch.

40

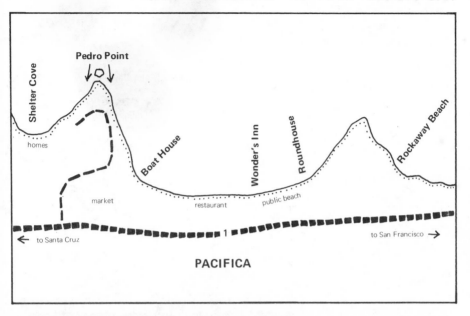

Cold but well-shaped peaks at the BOATHOUSE.

PACIFICA

A small coastal town a few miles south of San Francisco. Has incredible surf at the following spots:

Roundhouse

A temperamental peak. Mainly lefts-some rights. Best on a small, 2-6 foot west swell. Medium-low tide. Shape varies according to shifting sand bottom.

Wander's Inn

Shifting sandbar peaks. Lines are usually mushy but strong. Best on 2-6 foot west swells. Medium tide. Strong winter waves close out.

Boathouse

Winter beach peaks. Soft and easy from 2-4 feet. Steep and hardbreaking above that. A medium-low tide is best. Surfed when other spots close out. Breaks outside of old boathouse - south end of beach.

Pedro Point

A big wave break - winter only. Thick lefts (some rights) off north point of Shelter Cove. Needs a 6-15 foot swell and medium tide. **Note:** Rarely surfed . . . rocks and currents too dangerous!

41

CENTRAL CALIFORNIA

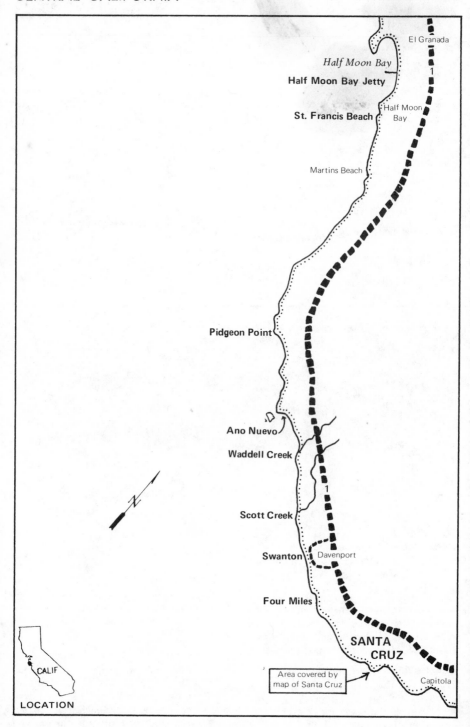

El Granada

Half Moon Bay

Half Moon Bay Jetty

St. Francis Beach

Half Moon Bay

1

Martins Beach

Pidgeon Point

Ano Nuevo

Waddell Creek

1

Scott Creek

Swanton Davenport

Four Miles

SANTA CRUZ

Capitola

Area covered by map of Santa Cruz

CALIF

LOCATION

Half Moon Bay Jetty

Thick, shifty beach peaks, $\frac{1}{4}$ mile below south jetty. Breaks year'round on any swell. Medium-low tide. Backwash off rocks at high tide. **Comment:** Unpredictable shape . . . a "hit or miss" spot.

St. Francis Beach

A sandy beach break, south of Half Moon Bay. Ridable on small, 1-4 foot swells. Medium tide. Strong lines usually close out. Never crowded.

Pidgeon Point

Long, right lines peeling off a rocky point. Needs a strong winter swell. Medium-low tide. **Comment:** Looks good but unmakeable sections are everywhere. Usually not worth the hassle.

Ano Nuevo

A clean summer break. Quick right tubes off north end of beach. Takes a 2-8 foot south swell. Medium-low tide. Usually glassy. Winter surf is small and bumpy.

The peaks of HALF MOON BAY.

Summer surf — WADDELL CREEK.

Riding high on the lip at FOUR MILES.

A big-wave reef somewhere between San Francisco and Santa Cruz.

The nasty rip at SCOTT CREEK.

Beach peaks below SCOTT CREEK.

Approaching the inside section of FOUR MILES.

Northwest swells peel across the outside reef at SCOTT CREEK. Note: Whitewater in foreground denotes the channel.

Waddell Creek

Smooth summer peaks along a wide, sandy beach. Needs a 2-8 foot south swell and medium tide. Center peaks are most often ridden. Never crowded . . . waves everywhere! Winter surf is big and unpredictable. **Note:** By summer, the sands have settled helping to produce clean, consistent shape.

Scott Creek

An explosive winter line. Peaks on a shallow reef and peels right. Then shoulders into deep water before it grinds across an inside ledge. Breaks on any winter swell from 2-12 feet. A strong north is best. Medium-low tide. Pounding shorebreak with strong downcoast currents. **Comment:** A strong wintertime break . . . respect its power.

The lineup at FOUR MILE — Although it looks inviting the outer point (middle right) is rarely surfed. The normal takeoff is to the left center of photo where smaller wave is breaking.

One of the many unsurfed reefs — Central California.

The shorebreak at FOUR MILE. Note size of wave compared to people. It's a good 6 feet.

SWANTON — Small lefts glisten in the afternoon sun. Location: the reef just south of the creek.

Swanton

Thick rights off the northern point. Peaks are shifty and inconsistent. Easy to get caught inside. Rarely surfed. **Also:** A peak left south of small creek. Both spots break on any swell from 2-8 feet. Medium tide. Easily blown out by northwest breezes.

Four Mile

Long, winter lines off a rocky point. Outer peak looks ridable . . . but isn't. Too shifty and unpredictable. The main peak is inside. A thick right that gradually works into a pounding shorebreak. Paddling channel south of breakline. Best in winter on a 2-10 foot swell. Medium-low tide. **Comment:** A powerful break that's never too crowded.

CENTRAL CALIFORNIA

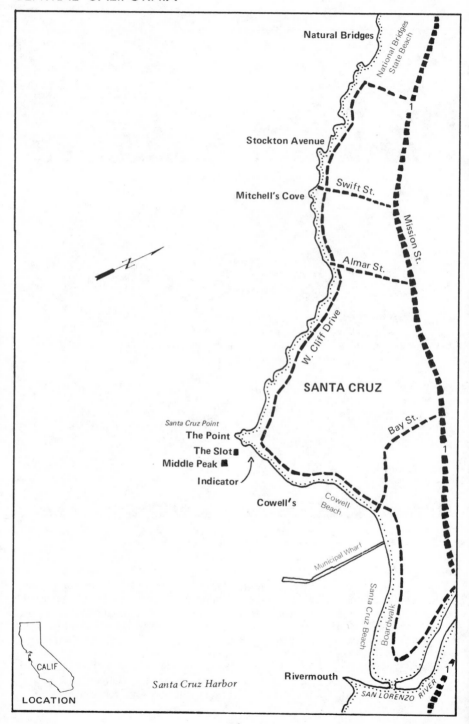

Natural Bridges

National Bridges State Beach

1

Stockton Avenue

Swift St.

Mitchell's Cove

Mission St.

Almar St.

W. Cliff Drive

SANTA CRUZ

Bay St.

Santa Cruz Point

The Point

The Slot

Middle Peak

1

Indicator

Cowell's

Cowell Beach

Municipal Wharf

Santa Cruz Beach

Boardwalk

Rivermouth

1

Santa Cruz Harbor

SAN LORENZO RIVER

CALIF

LOCATION

STEAMER LANE — Pictured above is the well known "Middle Peak" of Steamer's Lane. It breaks both summer and winter but attains its best size and shape during a strong northwest swell . . This photo was taken in February during a 6-8 foot west swell. The tide was medium-high. Compare this wave with the one on page 49. You can see how the tide affects both shape and speed. **Note:** Photo (page 49) was taken at medium-low tide.

CENTRAL CALIFORNIA

Lining it up at NATURAL BRIDGES.

Banking high into the soup of "Middle Peak" of STEAMER LANE.

Natural Bridges
A point-like right. Peaks over an outer reef and peels smoothly onto a wide sandy beach. Flat spots and tubular sections. Rock ledges in front of break. A winter spot . . . best on a 2-8 foot west swell. Medium-low tide.

Stockton Avenue
The best summer break in Santa Cruz. A steep peak followed by a thin right tube. Shallow reef. Kelp keeps chop down. Needs a 2-6 foot south swell with medium tide. **Comment:** A clean, summer tube.

Mitchell's Cove
The best shaped big wave in Santa Cruz. It pipes . . . bowls . . . and tubes. Breaks only 2-6 times a year. Needs a 12-20 foot winter swell. **Also:** Small rights in front of rock ledge. Needs a 2-6 foot winter swell. Medium-low tide.

Natural Bridges State Park.

STOCKTON AVENUE glass.

#2 The reef directs the swell into thick, concentrated peak producing steep vertical takeoffs. #3 Once the drop has been made, the wave demands a series of sweeping turns, climbs, and cutbacks, which are so important in Hawaiian surfing.

The magic ingredient that brings the Rivermouth to life is sand. Sand washed down the river by lots and lots of rain. For without rain there would be no sand and without sand Rivermouth would be just a big shorebreak.

STEAMER LANE — The "Middle Peak" of Steamer's Lane is one of California's best big-wave breaks. Oldtimers consider it as THEE spot to prepare for the Hawaiian Islands. The reasons: #1 It breaks almost 1/2mile from shore and requires a long swim for a lost board.

Pictured is a winter's blessing for the locals of Santa Cruz — the RIVERMOUTH is breaking. Tons of sand has accumulated at the mouth of the San Lorenzo River and formed a sandbar. Perfect two-way lines are peeling from a central peak. It doesn't get much better.

CENTRAL CALIFORNIA

Smooth winter lines explode off "The Point" of STEAMER LANE.

"Middle Peak" STEAMER LANE — This rider could have gone either way. He chose the left because today . . . it's got the juice!

STEAMER LANE

The center of surfing in Santa Cruz. Name refers to a series of reef breaks located along East Cliff Drive. All types of waves available: peaks, lines and shoulders. Breaks on any swell - year'-round. Best size and shape found during the winter months. Steep cliffs and a rocky shoreline await lost boards. Area breaks down as follows:

The Point

Powerful right walls off outermost point. Needs a 3-10 foot winter swell and medium-low tide. Too bumpy when tide is up. A steep, fast takeoff followed by a thick (sometimes hollow) line. Enter water from point, in front of light-house memorial. A winter break.

Middle Peak

The big wave spot of "The Lane". A steep, concentrated peak. Mushy, right shoulders and hollow, fast lefts. Starts to work around 6 feet — never closes out. As size increases peak moves further out. Breaks in summer too - but winter has the size and juice. **Caution:** Giant clean up sets are frequent . . . just part of the game!

Inside Peak / The Slot

A small peak located between The Point and Indicator. 100 yards inside Middle Peak. Clean rights that sometimes carry through Indicator. **Comment:** Very un-predictable . .. A right time, right place situation.

50

The lips are thick and the tubes can spit — STEAMER LANE.

Winter swells stack up at the "middle peak" — STEAMER LANE.

"Middle Peak" — at its best.

A kneerider slips under the lip as he moves from "The Slot" into "Indicator".

Indicator

A long, right wall . . . takes over when Middle Peak expires in a deep channel. Sometimes fast and hollow. Ridable from 2-8 feet. Medium-low tide. Works as a set indicator for Cowell's.

Cowell's

An excellent beginners break. Slow, easy right slides. Usually glassy. Takes a 2-6 foot north or west swell. Medium-low tide. Sand and rock bottom. **Comment:** One of the best learning spots in California.

Rivermouth

Peaks at the mouth of the San Lorenzo river. Perfection rights and lefts that peel and tube. Needs a 2-8 foot winter swell Medium-low tide. Breaks only after heavy rains when sandbars have had a chance to form. **Note:** Usually crowded . . . but well worth the effort.

51

CENTRAL CALIFORNIA

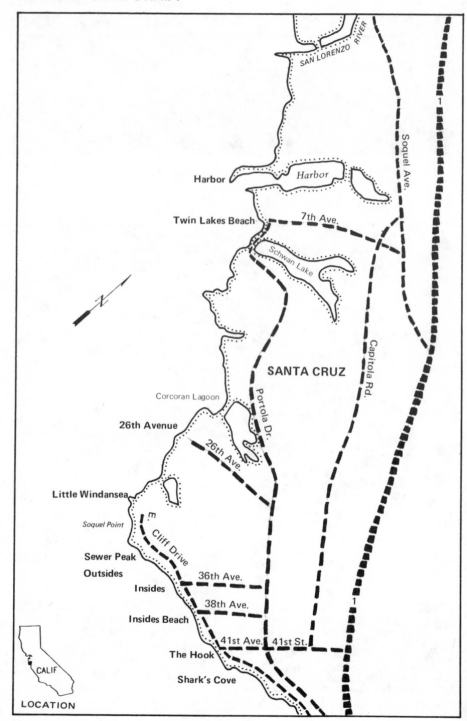

SAN LORENZO RIVER

Soquel Ave.

1

Harbor   *Harbor*

Twin Lakes Beach   7th Ave.

Schwan Lake

Capitola Rd.

SANTA CRUZ

Corcoran Lagoon

26th Avenue   26th Ave.

Portola Dr.

Little Windansea

Soquel Point

Cliff Drive

Sewer Peak

Outsides   36th Ave.

Insides   38th Ave.

Insides Beach

41st Ave. 41st St.

The Hook   1

Shark's Cove

CALIF

LOCATION

A clean right peels across the entrance to Santa Cruz Harbor.

Unusual shape at TWIN LAKES BEACH.

THE HARBOR: Large surf breaks at the end of the jetty. Small surf peels along the rocks and breaks inside the main channel (shown here).

Set'n it up at the HARBOR.

Harbor

Downcoast currents deposit sand along the north seawall creating right lines across harbor entrance. Takeoffs are steep with tubes to follow. Takes a 2-8 foot winter swell and low tide. On big swells rides past the second jetty are possible. Breaks every winter.

Twin Lakes Beach

A sand bottom beach break. Uncrowded because it's usually closed out. Sometimes after a storm . . . smooth peaks with hollow rights and lefts. **Comment:** A "sometimes" winter break.

Sand is being dredged from the Santa Cruz harbor. The waves in background will soon cease.

CENTRAL CALIFORNIA

26th Avenue — Santa Cruz.

26th Avenue
Shifty beach peaks. Either way. Works on any swell, 2-6 feet. Medium-high tide. Larger waves close out. Sand bottom and beach. Summer or winter.

Little Windansea
A fast left off outer reef. Just north of Pleasure Point. Best in early spring on a 3-8 foot west swell. Medium-low tide. **Caution:** Jagged, board-damaging rocks along shoreline.

Out of gas at PLEASURE POINT.

PLEASURE POINT
A series of reef breaks. Works year'-round. Best in winter when surf is big and strong. Steep cliffs and rocks along the shore. Thick kelp keeps the chop to a minimum. Area consists of the following breaks:

Sewer Peak
A crackling summer tube! Breaks top-to-bottom over a shallow rock reef. Takes any swell but best on a south. Ridable from 1-6 feet. Medium low tide. Gets name from nearby sewage outlet.

Dipping into a SEWER PEAK.

Outsides
Long, right lines off the outermost reef. Steep takeoffs with thick, roomy walls. Space for rolling and carving. Hot sections and flat spots everywhere. Takes any 3-10 foot swell and medium-low tide. A straight north is best . . . its got da juice! Summer and winter.

Insides
A smooth right. Takes over when Outsides expires in channel. Ridable from 2-6 feet, low tide. A favorite spot for long boarders . . . lots of "spinners" and "stretch fives". **Note:** On bigger swells right lines connect with ¼ mile rides possible.

LITTLE WIND'N SEA — It doesn't break very often but when it does it can get awfully good. The outline of the Monterey Peninsula can be seen in the background.

Inside's Beach
A beach wave. Needs a huge winter swell and low tide before it breaks. Never bigger than 5 feet. **Comment:** A "sometimes" spot.

Slashing through the crowd — the "outside" reef of Pleasure Point.

Turning back at PLEASURE POINT.

Re-entering the inside lineup at PLEASURE POINT.

PLEASURE POINT has all kinds of surf (see photos above). Slow waves, thick waves, fast and tubular waves. It's a very sensitive point break that needs a lot of help from Mother Nature. The wind, swell, and tide all have to work together before the surf attains quality. But when the point is on it's hard to beat.

CENTRAL CALIFORNIA

Winter swells peel into THE HOOK.

THE HOOK — A thick lip throws out as rider attempts to move under the inside section.

The HOOK throws out.

The Hook

A classic point break (see photo). Located at the end of 41st Ave. in Santa Cruz. Breaks on any swell — summer or winter. Best at medium-low tide. Gets name from the large amount of kelp in lineup. **Note:** Watch for the inside section that takes shape as the tide drops.

SHARK'S COVE — About as good as it gets.

THE HARBOR — During winter months, sand accumulates along the north seawall of the Santa Cruz Harbor. These sandbars produce constant surf that breaks at the mouth of the entrance (see above). In this photo a small motorboat guns for the open sea as 5 foot set explodes to the right.

Shark's Cove
A continuation of The Hook. Peaks off outer point then wraps into cove. A winter wave, ridable from 2-8 feet. Low tide. Thick kelp. **Comment:** A speed wave that wraps . . . peels . . . and tubes.

SHARK'S COVE.

CENTRAL CALIFORNIA

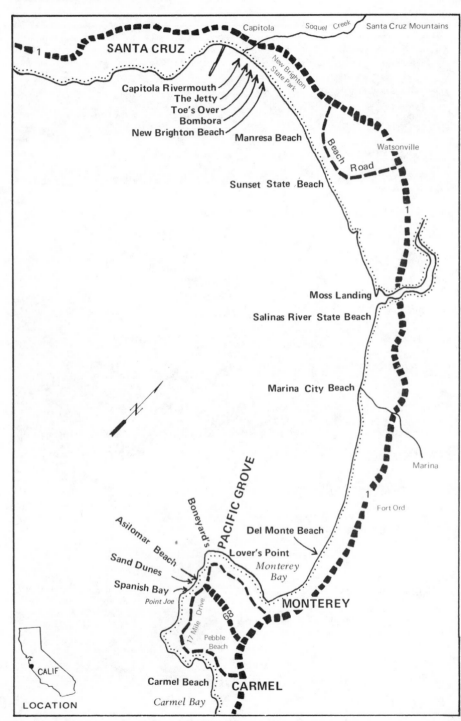

1

SANTA CRUZ

Capitola

Soquel Creek

Santa Cruz Mountains

New Brighton State Park

Capitola Rivermouth
The Jetty
Toe's Over
Bombora
New Brighton Beach

Manresa Beach

Watsonville

Beach

Road

1

Sunset State Beach

Moss Landing

Salinas River State Beach

Marina City Beach

Marina

N

PACIFIC GROVE

1

Fort Ord

Boneyard's

Asilomar Beach

Del Monte Beach

Sand Dunes

Lover's Point

Spanish Bay

Monterey Bay

Point Joe

MONTEREY

68

17 Mile Drive

Pebble Beach

CALIF

Carmel Beach

CARMEL

LOCATION

Carmel Bay

Capitola Rivermouth
Tubular sandbar peaks - right and left. Needs a huge winter swell before it breaks. Medium-low tide. Never gets above 4 feet. Inconsistent shape - depends on the contour of the sand bottom. **Comment:** Not heavily surfed . . . a "sometimes" spot.

The Jetty
Short but fast rights off a small rock groin. Needs a big winter swell and minus low tide. A private break for the locals of Capitola.

Toe's Over
Smooth peaks with soft shoulders. Needs a huge winter swell and minus low tide. Rarely gets bigger than 4 feet. Thick kelp keeps it glassy. Never crowded . . . South of the Capitola pier.

Bombora
Glass-smooth lefts from a central peak. Shallow reef. Breaks only on the biggest winter swells. Needs a minus low tide. Rarely gets above 2-3 feet. **Comment:** Never crowded. . .off the beaten track.

CAPITOLA — The surf here is usually flat all year. Once in awhile the reefs and beaches come to life and generate surf like that seen above (Capitola Pier) and below (Bombora). For more information see descriptions on top of this page.

Located about 1/2 mile below the Capitola Pier is a small reef named BOMBORA. It needs a large winter swell and a minus low tide before it will break (which isn't often). When it does it resembles the photo above.

CENTRAL CALIFORNIA

New Brighton Beach
Gentle rights off small point reef. Needs a big winter swell and minus low tide. Thick kelp. Sandy beach. An excellent beginners break. **Note:** Camping allowed in state park.

Manresa Beach
A high-powered beach break. Takes any swell. Medium tide. Ridable from 2-6 feet. Larger surf holds shape but getting outside is almost impossible. Sandy beach and bottom. **Caution:** Massive rip currents during large swells - surfing very chancy!

Tight squeeze at MANRESA BEACH.

Sunset State Beach
A potent break - summer and winter. Strong swells focus onto this beach producing well-shaped peaks and lines. Ridable from 2-6 feet. Above that and it gets hairy. Rarely ridden. **Note.** Camping allowed in state park.

MARINA BEACH — big and gnarly.

Moss Landing
Quality peaks along miles of undeveloped beachfront. Main peak is just north of jetty. Top-to-bottom takeoffs with long, pumping tubes. Takes a north or west swell, 2-8 feet. Medium tide. Best after a storm . . . when offshores blow out of the Salinas Valley. **Comment:** Locals are hostile ... visitors take heed.

CAPITOLA RIVERMOUTH.

MOSS LANDING

MOSS LANDING — Big and round with perfect shape.

The shark infested waters of SALINAS RIVER STATE BEACH.

SUNSET STATE BEACH — Thundering winter swells pour across the outer sandbar. Note: Although its well-shaped, surf is usually too big and consistent.

Salinas River State Beach

Rarely surfed sandbar peaks. Breaks on any swell from 2-6 feet. Medium tide. Sandy beach and bottom. **Caution:** Deep water and refuse attract sharks. . . . keep eyes peeled.

Marina City Beach

A seldom seen beach break. Works year'round but is rarely ridden. Best from 2-6 feet, medium tide. Winter surf is usually too big and dangerous. Summer months are calm and safe.

The long north lines of ASILOMAR BEACH.

The jagged shoreline of Pacific Grove.

BONEYARD'S — about to peel.

LOVER'S POINT.

Del Monte Beach

Beach surf . . . usually walled up. Bottom drops off sharply creating almost constant shorebreak. Sandy beach and bottom. Good swimming during warm summer months.

Lover's Point

A left off a rocky point. Easy takeoffs with thick, wide shoulders. Room to climb and carve. Needs a winter swell, 3-8 feet. Medium-low tide. Small waves break onto rocks. **Comment:** The main surf break for the locals of Pacific Grove.

Boneyard's

Dangerous lefts in front of a jagged shoreline. A winter break. Ridable from 2-8 feet. Medium-high tide a must! Rock boils everywhere. **Comment:** Never crowded . . . and for good reason.

Asilomar Beach

Consistent surf along a ½ mile of sandy beach. Two ridable peaks separated by a deep paddling channel. Breaks on any swell from 1-8 feet. Winter has the juice! Medium tide usually produces the best shape. Reliable offshore winds. **Note:** A popular tourist beach. Located between Carmel and Pacific Grove.

Early morning at ASILOMAR BEACH.

Sand Dunes
Clean blue-water peaks. Shifting rights and lefts over a sand bottom. Takes any swell from 2-8 feet. Winter best. Medium-high tide. **Note:** A short hike from Asilomar.

Spanish Bay
½ mile of smooth beach surf. Shifting peaks breaking into crystal blue water. Any swell. Medium-low tide. Sandy beach and bottom. Never crowded. **Note:** Located along 17 mile drive . . . Save $3.00 and walk from Asilomar Beach.

Strong offshores hold up the winter lines at SPANISH BAY.

Carmel Beach
Shifting peaks along a mile of public beach. Steep takeoffs and quicks tubes. Cracking shorebreak. Sandy beach and bottom. Works on any swell from 1-5 feet. Medium tide usually best. **Note:** This is the central beach of Carmel . . . a very mellow town.

CARMEL BEACH — Small peaks like the break all along Carmel's main beach.

CENTRAL CALIFORNIA

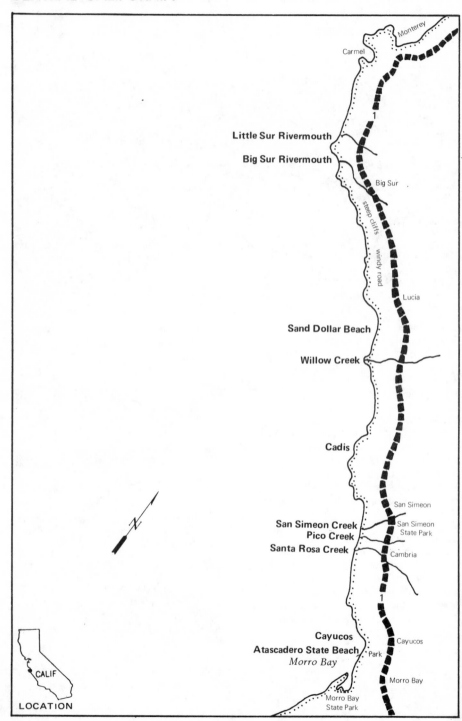

Little Sur Rivermouth

Pop up peaks at rivers end. Shape is inconsistent - depends on flow of sand from river. A winter break. **Note:** Rarely surfed . . . but always worth a look.

Big Sur Rivermouth

Flawless lines that peel and tube into a rivermouth channel. Lefts and rights. Breaks on any swell from 2-12 feet. Medium-low tide. Normal breezes blow offshore. **Note:** A short ¼ mile hike across private property.

Sand Dollar Beach

Powerful winter walls. Starts working at 2 feet and **never** closes out. Deep side channels provide safe access to peaks. Massive rip currents. **Comment:** Reports of 25 foot peaks . . . smooth and ridable!

Willow Creek

Beach peaks. Size and power are very deceptive. Breaks from 3-12 feet, any winter swell. Medium-low tide. Super cold water. Smooth cobblestones await lost boards. **Comment:** Surf looks soft and mellow . . . but isn't!

Winter peaks at WILLOW CREEK.

BIG SUR RIVERMOUTH.

The "north peak" — SAND DOLLAR BEACH.

The "south peak" — SAND DOLLAR BEACH.

WILLOW CREEK — The waves here are deceptive. They appear soft but break with awesome force.

One of the virginal reefs at CADIS.

Winter lines stack onto another CADIS reef.

A guardhouse stands lonely vigil over a perfect CADIS wall.

Cadis

Perfection tubes along a mile of untouched beach. Clean rights and lefts off outer reefs. Breaks on any swell from 2-10 feet. Medium-low tide. Winter surf is usually too big and bumpy. Summer months are best. Prevailing winds are offshore! **Note:** Area is fenced . . . but an easy walk across a grassy cow pasture.

San Simeon Creek

Thin, fast lines off the north point. Usually unmakeable. Also: Sandbar peaks along beach. Shape varys according to changing sand bottom. Works from 2-6 feet, medium-low tide. Mainly a winter break but has small summer surf too. **Note:** Camping allowed in state park (across Hwy 1).

Two-way peaks at PICO CREEK.

An oil pier — north of MORRO BAY.

Crisp lines at the SANTA ROSA CREEK.

A longboard shooter — CAYUCOS.

Beach lines — ATASCADERO.

Pico Creek

A soft peak south of the creek. Easy rights and lefts. Takes any winter swell. Best from 2-6 feet. Medium tide. Located in front of hotels along Hwy 1. **Comment:** Shape depends on flow of sand from river. A winter break.

Santa Rosa Creek

Two way lines from a central peak. Ridable from 2-6 feet — any winter swell. Medium-low tide. Shape changes daily . . . usually good after heavy rains. **Comment:** A "hit or miss spot" - but always worth a look.

Cayucos

Slow, easy lefts. South side of pier. Takes any swell, 1-5 feet. Medium-high tide. Sandy beach and bottom. **Comment:** A weekend favorite for long boarders.

Atascadero Sate Beach

Clean beach lines. Needs good weather and a 2-5 foot swell. Medium-low tide. Sand beach and bottom. Never crowded . . . few surfers in area. **Note:** Camping allowed in state park.

CENTRAL CALIFORNIA

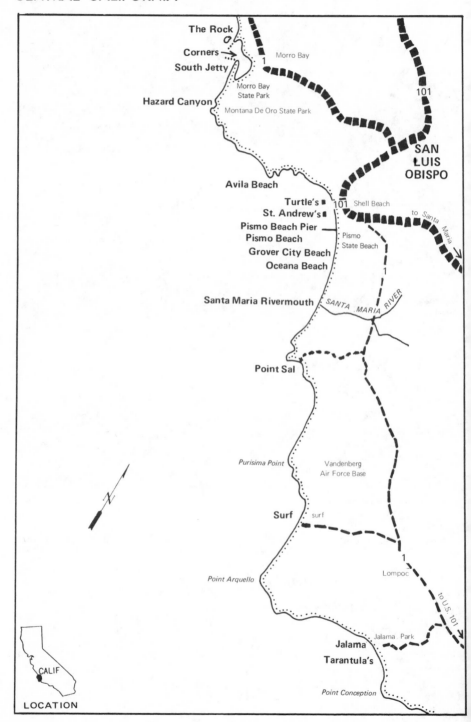

The Rock
Corners
South Jetty
Morro Bay
1
Morro Bay State Park
Montana De Oro State Park
Hazard Canyon
101
SAN LUIS OBISPO
Avila Beach
Turtle's
St. Andrew's
101
Shell Beach
to Santa Maria
Pismo Beach Pier
Pismo Beach
Pismo State Beach
Grover City Beach
Oceana Beach
1
Santa Maria Rivermouth
SANTA MARIA RIVER
Point Sal
Purisima Point
Vandenberg Air Force Base
Surf
surf
1
Point Arquello
Lompoc
to U.S. 101
Jalama Park
Jalama
Tarantula's
Point Conception
CALIF
LOCATION

The Rock
Two way peaks off outer sand bars. Best on small, 2-5 foot swells. Medium tide. Hard to get out during bigger surf. Located north of the famous "Morro Rock". **Comment:** A consistent break — summer and winter.

THE ROCK — Morro Bay.

Corners
Pocket lefts breaking 15 feet from rocks. A constant tube peeling along inside of jetty. Breaks from 2-6 feet. Low tide. **Also:** Long lefts in the middle of the bay. Needs a large winter swell and low tide. A "Pipeline" left . . . but doesn't happen too often.

South Jetty
Two way lines from a main peak. Needs a 2-8 foot winter swell. Medium-low tide. Isolated . . . reached by paddling across main channel and around seawall. **Caution:** Rip currents and sharks.

SOUTH JETTY — Morro Bay.

Crisp, early mornings lines at THE ROCK.

Pictured above is the south seawall of Morro Bay. To the extreme left are the lines of SOUTH JETTY. In the center of photo — breaking along the inside of the jetty — are the fast tubes of CORNERS. To the extreme right are the faint showings of another left which only breaks during the biggest of winter swells.

CENTRAL CALIFORNIA

AVILA BEACH — Glassy peaks at the San Luis Rivermouth.

Low tide lines at PISMO BEACH.

Hazard Canyon
Thick peaks across a jagged reef. Works on a 3-8 foot winter swell. Medium tide. A dangerous break — rarely ridden. Located inside Montana De Oro State Park . . . camping allowed.

Avila Beach
Glassy, two way peaks. Breaks at the foot of the San Luis rivermouth. Takes any winter swell, 2-6 feet. Best after heavy rains when sandbars have had a chance to form. **Note:** Summer surf is nothing . . . just shorebreak.

Turtles
Easy beginners surf. Breaks all year. Any swell, 1-5 feet. Medium tide. Slow mushy lines . . . perfect for young surfers. 2 miles above Shell Beach in front of private homes.

TURTLES is the main surf spot of Shell Beach. During big swells it breaks like the Sunset Cliffs in San Diego.

St. Andrews
The main break of Shell Beach. Needs a 3-10 foot swell. Medium tide. Big and strong during large swells. Soft and slow when small. Rocks and cliffs inside . . . leashes advisable. On Seacrest Drive, just off Hwy 1.

70

Two lone surfers head into the PT. SAL lineup.

A liney west swell wraps into the lee of PT. SAL. The cove (lower right) is the main surf break. The rest of the point is yet untried.

A lone rider boogies off the bottom as he tries to avoid a thick section—POINT SAL.

Pismo Beach Pier
Beach peaks on both sides of pier. South side is favored. Breaks year'-round from 2-5 feet. Medium tide. Sandy bottom . . . shape is unpredictable. **Comment:** Best bet . . . evening glass offs.

Pismo / Grover / and Oceana Beach
Wide sandy beaches. Sandbar peaks ¼ mile offshore. Countless lines of soup . . . hard to get out. Breaks on any swell. Medium tide. **Comment:** Rarely surfed . . . not worth the paddle.

Santa Maria Rivermouth
Sandbar peaks breaking ¼ mile out. Takes any swell, 2-6 feet. Medium tide. Surf is gnarly and usually closed out. Shifting sand bottom — shape is unpredictable. Best during the calm summer months.

Point Sal
Countless reef breaks along a jutting point of land (photo). Only one break is ridden . . . it's a thick, peak takeoff wth a powerful right wall. Ends in an exploding shorebreak. Needs a 3-10 foot west swell. Medium-low tide. **Note:** A twisting dirt road leads off Hwy 1 to the undeveloped Point Sal Beach Park. **Caution:** Road washes out when it rains . . . which is often.

CENTRAL CALIFORNIA

The shoreline between Jalama County Park and Point Conception is still in its natural state. It is also privately owned and entry is prohibited . . . Pictured above are just two of countless reef breaks found along this coastline. Waves break year'round with Point Conception best in winter and Jalama best in summer. **Note:** Area is reached by walking south from Jalama Park along the beach. But keep an eye on the tide. Many points become impassible at high tide. Use utmost caution — help is a long ways off.

Surf
Miles of sandbar beach peaks. Breaks on any swell from 2-6 feet. Medium tide. Winter surf is big and usually closed out. **Comment:** Best in summer when it's calm and safe.

Jalama
A primo summer break. Big lefts that spit and chew. Needs a 2-10 foot south swell. Medium tide. Sand bottom and beach. 48 miles north of Santa Barbara, off Hwy 1. **Note:** Camping allowed in this county park.

Tarantula's
Winter lefts off an outer reef. Breaks on a north or west swell, 2-8 feet. Medium-low tide. **Comment:** Strong, uncrowded walls. A short walk south of Jalama County Park.

THE AREA: This section covers the well known and crowded south coast of California. It extends from Point Conception to the Mexican Border. For a detailed map refer to page 6.

THE LAND: At one time the Southern California coast encompassed some of the most beautiful yet rugged shoreline in all the world. Fertile ranchlands, mellow green valleys, and white sand beaches were everywhere . . . A virgin paradise — awaiting discovery. Well, time and progress has changed all that. People moved west. Towns sprang up and started to grow. And today, almost 100 years later, they're still growing. Some say it's not far off when "solid city" will extend from Santa Barbara to San Diego. And what does the future hold — it's anybody's guess.

THE PEOPLE: Southern California is still growing. It's expanding north and south. People are everywhere — especially along the coast and in the water. During a good size swell it's common to see 40-75 boards at one break. And it's getting worse. As the population continues to expand so does the number of surfers. And sadly . . . there is no end in sight.

WATER TEMPERATURE: Favorable conditions prevail year'round. In winter, the water ranges from 55 degrees to 57 degrees — wetsuits are recommended. Boots, sleeves, and gloves are not necessary. During summer, the temperature moves into the 60°s and sometimes into the 70°s. — Wetsuits aren't necessary but they protect you from the hordes of jellyfish.

ACCESS: Only a small portion of the south coast is open to the public. Miles and miles of private property and military bases restrict access. Hundreds of beaches and surfing spots are used by only a few while public facilities are over crowded . . . But times are changing. As demand for beachfront increases so does the cry for accessibility. Surfing beaches that were once private (i.e. San Onofre, Trestle, Topanga Cyn.) are now public. Right-a-ways are being cut where home owners once had fences. How fast this happens depends on the demands and involvement of the beach-loving public.

CAMPING: For an area as large and as populated as this coastline, camping facilities are horribly inadequate. There are only 12 beach parks between Point Conception and Mexico that allow overnight camping. The demand for space is so great that reservations have to be made months in advance . . . The outlook is bleak. Even though the population continues to expand, the number of parks stays the same. Only the following allow camping:

> Gaviota State Beach
> Refugio State Beach
> El Capitan State Beach
> Carpinteria State Beach
> Emma Wood State Beach
> McGrath State Beach
> Leo Carrillo State Beach
> Doheny State Beach
> San Clemente State Beach
> San Onofre State Park
> South Carlsbad State Beach
> San Elijo State Beach

SOUTHERN CALIFORNIA

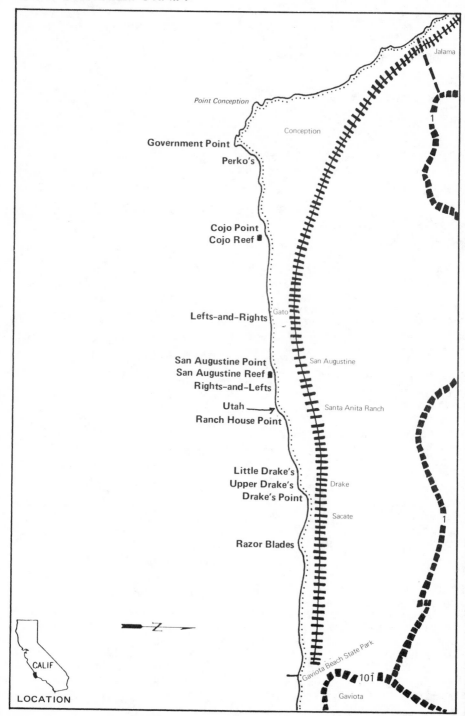

Point Conception

Conception

Jalama

1

Government Point

Perko's

Cojo Point
Cojo Reef ▪

Lefts-and-Rights — Gato

San Augustine Point
San Augustine Reef ▪
Rights-and-Lefts

San Augustine

Utah →
Ranch House Point

Santa Anita Ranch

Little Drake's
Upper Drake's
Drake's Point

Drake

Sacate

Razor Blades

1

N

Gaviota Beach State Park

10î ▪

CALIF
LOCATION

Gaviota

Evening glass at RIGHTS & LEFTS. The rights are perfect as they peel into the channel. The tide is out and the lefts are closing out. "Ranch boats" can be seen milling outside.

An odd looking pontoon boat lies in anchor at Cojo Point as fierce winds roar offshore.

Government Point

Long, right lines that peel and tube off a rocky point. Breaks year'round and is usually smooth and well-shaped. Best during a strong well lined north swell. Ridable from 2 feet up. Medium-low tide. **Note:** Winter surf only.

Perko's

Slow rights off a small point. Initial drop is steep but is followed by a flat, powerless shoulder. Wave ends in a strong shorebreak. Takes a south swell from 2-6 feet.

Cojo Point

One of the best summer waves on the ranch. Fast rights that break over a rocky shelf and peel smoothly to shore. Best during a strong south swell from 2-15 feet. Medium-low tide. **Caution:** Watch for pounding shorebreak during heavy surf. **Note:** Winter surf doesn't have the shape.

Cojo Reef

Lines focus onto an outside reef and form a central peak with both right and left shoulders. Waves are almost always soft and mushy. Never breaks hard. Works on any swell — summer or winter. **Never** closes out.

COJO POINT has the best summer surf on the Ranch. It's a long boat ride from Gaviota Park and therefore never very crowded. During strong south swells, long tapered lines peel for nearly a ¼ mile. Depending on the tide, a Cojo wave can be either soft and easy or fast and tubular. These photos were taken at medium-high tide and the shape is perfect. You can imagine what it's like at low tide. **Note:** The land to the right is Point Conception. It acts as a natural buffer against winds and provides Cojo with smooth conditions nearly all the time.

San Augustine Point.

Lost power on takeoff — RIGHTS & LEFTS.

COJO POINT.

A belly full of RIGHTS & LEFTS.

Lefts and Rights
A rock reef with both lefts and rights peeling off a central peak. Ridable from 2-6 feet. Best at a medium-low tide. Works on both a west or a south swell.

San Augustine Point
A small peak break off the outer point (see map). Rights and lefts that are ridable from 2-6 feet. Works on any southerly swell. Medium tide.

San Augustine Reef
A steep, hollow peak that quickly backs off in deep water. Breaks both left and right - rights best. Works on any winter swell from 2 feet and up. Medium-high tide. Located just south of San Augustine Point.

Rights and Lefts
Clean, two-way lines across a small outer reef. An easy takeoff followed by a well-shaped right or left tube. Takes a west swell and is ridable from 2-6 feet. Any tide is OK but medium-low is usually best. **Comment:** Usually crowded . . . the first place everyone checks.

One of a priviledged few.

Head down and movin toward the channel.

RIGHTS & LEFTS is the most consistent and also the most crowded spot on the Ranch. It receives both summer and winter swells and always seems to have surf. The rights are usually better than the lefts and these photos will prove why: #1 The takeoff: steep and fast. Rider has barely turned and he's already in the tube. Note the left on extreme right side of picture. It's working too but not as well. #2 He's still inside as the wave explodes toward the channel. #3 The wave has lost some size but none of its shape. #4 As the wave enters deep water it suddenly "backs off" requiring a quick cutback. #5 (not shown) Rider paddles back to lineup and the whole process repeats . . . An average day at RIGHTS & LEFTS.

Turning high off a "Ranch" lip.

A human seaweed slasher.

Cojo: what more could you ask for.

Offshore smoke — COJO POINT.

Utah
A peak right. Breaks in summer on any south swell. Ridable to 6 feet. Located in front of a rugged canyon mouth just below rights and lefts.

Ranch House Point
A misleading point break. South swells wrap onto point and peel smoothly to shore. Waves look makeable but usually aren't. Too many sections and wide flat spots. Works on any south swell from 2-8 feet. **Comment:** Seldom surfed . . . too many better spots.

Little Drake's
A hairball right. Peak sucks out across a shallow rock shelf and grinds either right or left. Works on any winter swell. Starts to smoke around 8 feet.

Upper Drake's
A small peak that breaks outside of Drake's Point. Only ridable from 2-6 feet then closes across to point. Works on any winter swell from 2-6 feet. Medium tide.

Drake's Point
One of the best point breaks on the ranch. Long rights that peel smoothly off a rocky point. Always clean and well-shaped. Works on any winter swell from 3-15 feet. Medium-low tide. **Note:** Spits and grinds at low tide.

Razor Blades
The first ridable spot as you boat into the Ranch. Smooth rights off a point. Breaks on any winter swell from 3-10 feet. Medium tide a must! **Caution:** Sharp, jagged rocks await lost boards — use a leash.

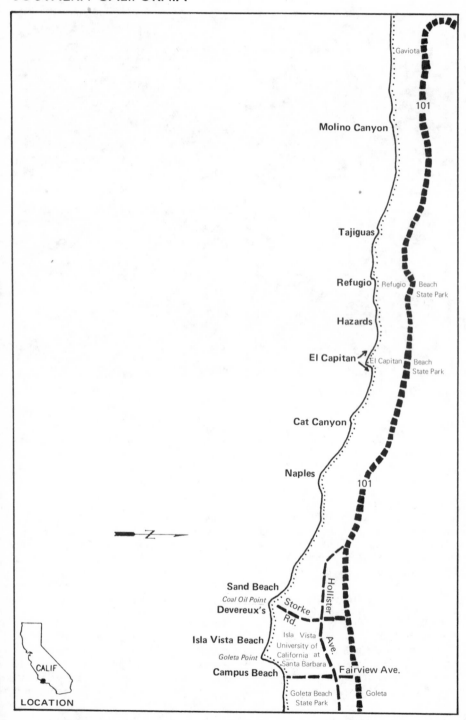

The inside of MOLINO CANYON.

The outer point — MOLINO CANYON.

A thick shoulder peels into the channel — TAJIGUAS.

TAJIGUAS — the winter lineup.

Molino Canyon

An isolated point break. Clean right lines off a central peak. Tubular inside section. Takes any winter swell, 2-6 ft. Medium-low tide. Steep cliffs and rocks along shoreline. **Comment:** Just south of Getty Oil . . . a narrow trail leads to beach.

Tajiguas

A private break. A central peak with clean right and left lines. Takes a 2-6 foot winter swell. Medium-low tide. Channel Islands block south swells. Best in early spring. **Comment:** Respect the rights of this small beachfront community . . . enter from public beaches to the north or south.

Refugio

A mellow, semi-point break. Steep take-offs with slow right lines. Becomes thick and mushy as swell gets bigger. Breaks from 2-6 feet on any winter swell. Best at medium-low tide. **Note:** Public camping allowed at this woodsy beach park. **Comment:** Easy surf, no hazards . . . a nice place to learn.

SOUTHERN CALIFORNIA

Going backside . . . REFUGIO STATE PARK.

HAZARDS. The "inside" reef at medium tide.

The "point" at HAZARDS. A lost board means trouble.

HAZARDS

A short stretch of sand and rock a few miles below Refugio State Park. Three spots yield winter surf:

The Point: Long, tubular rights off a rocky point. Breaks from 2-6 feet - any winter swell. Medium-low tide. Jagged shoreline - use a leash.

Middles: Mild peaks with easy rights onto a sandy beach. Takes same swell as The Point. Needs a low tide before it cooks.

Insides: Smooth two-way peaks off a small reef. Ridable from 2-5 feet - then closes out. Medium-low tide. Becomes tubular as tide drops. Ends in pounding shorebreak. A winter break.

A small day at "the point" of EL CAPITAN. Most winter swells pass by having little or no effect. Only during a large, very west swell will it reach maximum potential.

West Lines wrap around "The Point" of EL CAPITAN . . . The tide is low and the rocks prove it. Everyone is riding the outer point because the surf is slightly bigger. The inside lineup is well-shaped but small and too shallow. **Note:** During large surf (6-10 feet) and the right tide, waves are sometimes makeable from outer point to the beach inside — a ¼ mile.

EL CAPITAN

One of California's most natural settings for surfing or camping. Two spots produce winter surf:

The Beach: Small peaks with two-way lines. Best on a 2-5 foot winter swell. Incoming high tide. Bigger waves close out. Sandy beach and bottom. Located in front of main parking lot.

The Point: A classic point break (photo). Endless right tubes that peel and spit for miles. Needs a huge winter swell before it breaks. West swells are best. Top-to-bottom at low tide. Rocky shoreline and beach. **Comment:** A super-long tube . . . not always makeable but worth a try. **Note:** Camping allowed in this earthy beach park.

A transparent lip hooks into SAND BEACH.

The inside section at DEVEREUX'S.

Cat Canyon

A sizable right off a rocky point. Ridable from 4-8 feet, west swell. Private property - requires a 4 mile hike from El Capitan. **Comment:** Rarely worth the effort.

Naples

Small beach peaks. Ridable from 1-4 feet. Best after a storm on a peaky west swell. Medium tide. **Comment:** Only ridden by the locals of this small, beachfront community.

Sand Beach

Thick, tubular beach walls. Breaks from 2-10 feet on any winter swell. Consistent shape due to the hard rock and sand bottom. Medium-low tide usually best. **Note:** Enter from Isla Vista beach and walk north around Coal Oil Point. **Comment:** Miles of uncrowded tubes.

Devereux's

Various reef breaks along a ½ mile of Coal Oil Point. Mainly rights - some lefts. Outer peaks are steep and fast. Inside peaks are mild and soft-breaking . . . good for beginners. Needs a 2-10 foot winter swell and medium tide. Rock and sand bottom. Usually glassy. **Note:** Named after the private school on the bluffs above. **Comment:** Never that crowded - plenty of room for everybody.

Isla Vista Beach

Well-shaped beach peaks and lines. Best on a strong 3-8 foot winter swell when peaks form on reefs 300 yds. offshore. Medium-low tide is best. **Comment:** Doesn't break very hard but rides are super long and it's never crowded.

DEVEREUX'S (Coal Oil Point).

A mellow line — ISLA VISTA BEACH.

A "secret spot" south of TAJIGUAS.

A "point" wave — CAMPUS BEACH.

The "poles" lineup — CAMPUS BEACH.

The outer point of REFUGIO PARK.

CAMPUS BEACH

A sheltered point break on the campus of U.C.S.B. Used mainly by the students and faculty. The surf doesn't exactly thunder but it does offer relief from the hassles of college life. There are three distinct surfing breaks:

The Point: Well-shaped rights off a rocky point. Breaks only in winter from 2-8 ft. Medium-low tide waves are sometimes fast and tubular. Rocks along shore.

Poles: Lines peak near old pilings and peel right and left. Usually are soft and slowbreaking. Best from 2-6 feet. Medium-low tide.

Insides: Small, well-shaped rights that peel smoothly in front of a sandy beach. Never gets very big. Few hazards. A good beginners break.

SOUTHERN CALIFORNIA

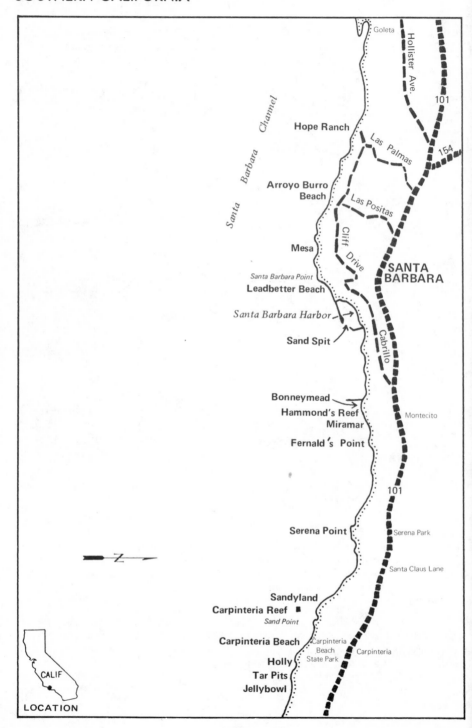

Goleta

Hollister Ave.

101

Santa Barbara Channel

Hope Ranch

Las Palmas

154

Arroyo Burro
Beach

Las Positas

Mesa

Cliff Drive

SANTA
BARBARA

Santa Barbara Point

Leadbetter Beach

Santa Barbara Harbor

Sand Spit

Cabrillo

Bonneymead

Hammond's Reef
Miramar

Montecito

Fernald's Point

101

Serena Point

Serena Park

Santa Claus Lane

Sandyland

Carpinteria Reef ■

Sand Point

Carpinteria Beach

Carpinteria
Beach
State Park

Carpinteria

Holly

Tar Pits

Jellybowl

N

CALIF

LOCATION

Hope Ranch

A private stretch of coastline. Only accessible to members and guests of ranch. Uncrowded points and beach breaks. Works on any winter swell from 2-8 feet. Medium tide. **Note:** The Channel Islands block south swells — very little surf during summer months.

Arroyo Burro Beach

Typical sand bottom beach break. Small peaks with short rights and lefts. Ridable from 1-4 feet - any winter swell. Medium tide. **Note:** Best shape during a peaky wind swell.

Mesa

A "hard to find" reef break. Always has surf and is never too crowded. Works 2-5 feet - any winter swell. Rocks everywhere . . . medium-high tide a must. Kelp helps keep it glassy. **Comment:** A popular spot for the locals of area.

Leadbetter Beach

Various reef formations generate soft right slides in front of a rock point. Easy takeoffs with mild lines. Takes any winter swell from 2-8 feet. Low tide. **Comment:** An excellent break for beginners and longboard holdouts.

Inaccessible waves — HOPE RANCH.

The hard to find waves of MESA.

LEADBETTORS BEACH. Easy waves . . . good for beginners.

A west swell rolls through at HAMMOND'S. Note consistency of height and thickness.

SOUTHERN CALIFORNIA

West swells stack into HAMMOND'S REEF.

Jamming beneath the inside section at HAMMOND'S.

Sand Spit

Long perfect tubes when its working. Breaks in front of a sandy peninsula near the entrance to Santa Barbara harbor. Needs a strong winter swell and low tide. Usually 2-3 feet smaller than other breaks. **Comment:** A "super **tube"** if you can catch it.

Bonneymead

Summer: Fast lefts on the south side of the pier. Needs a 2-5 foot south swell. Large boulders on beach - low tide is a must.

Winter: Thick right walls . . . sometimes makeable. Works on any winter swell from 2-8 feet. Shape best on a west. Rocks and boulders along beach. Medium low tide a must. **Comment:** Waves are big and strong. No place for a beginner.

Hammond's Reef

Mr. Hammond's estate has been torn down . . . condominiums have been built . . . but the green lawn and waves are still there.

Long rights (some lefts) off a semipoint. Steep takeoffs followed by thick, well-shaped line up. Large section appears quickly then backs off allowing room for driving cutbacks. Then gains speed as it moves across inside reef. Ride ends as wave nears shore. Takes any winter swell from 3-15 feet. Medium tide. **Comment:** One of the best winter spots in all of Santa Barbara County.

Note: The estate is threatened. Land developers want to build apartments atop the grassy knoll.

A big set unwinds across HAMMOND'S REEF. Note increasing size of surf from bottom to top. Number 4 wave is the biggest.

Miramar

Small rights off a rocky point just north of hotel. Ridable from 1-4 feet on any winter swell. Low tide best. Rock bottom/sandy beach. **Comment:** A good beginners break - safe and easy to ride.

Fernald's Point

Tiny peaks with short right slides. Picks up most swells - summer and winter. Beach is private but is heavily used during summer months. **Comment:** Poorly shaped. most of time . . . usually not worth checking.

Serena Point

A private surf break. Little rights off a rocky point. Occasional peaks across the inside reef. Usually small and very sectiony. Needs a strong winter swell and medium tide. **Note:** Enter from public beach at Summerland.

Sandyland

Beach surf for the locals of Carpinteria. Takes any swell from 1-5 feet. A peaky west swell is best. Larger surf closes out. Sand beach and bottom. 1 mile above Carpinteria.

Carpinteria Reef

Bumpy, irregular peaks breaking over a shallow reef that extends $\frac{1}{4}$ from shore. Needs a big clean winter swell. Small surf is dangerous. **Comment:** Rarely attains ridable quality - a "sometimes" spot.

Carpinteria Beach

Routine beach surf. Breaks on any swell and ridable from 1-5 feet. Anything bigger and it closes out. Shape best at medium-high tide. **Note:** Camping permitted in State Park.

Holly

Rights and lefts across outer reefs. Unmakable sections everywhere. Very slow and very mushy. Takes any swell but rarely any good. **Comment:** Surfed by locals of area and that's about all.

Tar Pits

Easy peaks breaking over a rock and clay bottom. Works on any swell. It seems to be always bumpy or blown out.

Jelly Bowl

Inconsistent peaks - $\frac{1}{4}$ mile above old pier. Best during summer months on a 1-6 foot south swell. Winter waves are either too bumpy or closed out. **Comment:** A private break for the locals of South Carpinteria.

SOUTHERN CALIFORNIA

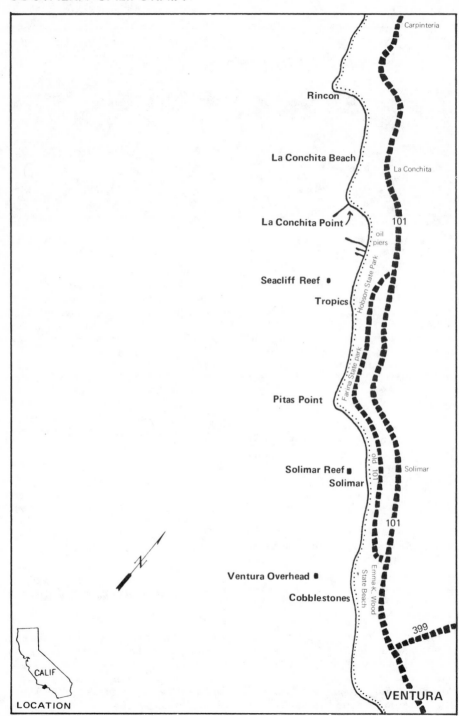

Carpinteria

Rincon

La Conchita Beach

La Conchita

La Conchita Point

101

oil piers

Seacliff Reef

Hobson State Park

Tropics

Farina State Park

Pitas Point

Solimar Reef

old 101

Solimar

Solimar

101

Ventura Overhead

Emma K. Wood State Beach

Cobblestones

399

CALIF

LOCATION

N

VENTURA

RINCON. Smooth northern lines peel off the "first point".

Three longboards wait for a lull as a big set rolls through at the "First Point". RINCON . . . early 1960.

RINCON POINT

Considered by most as one of the best winter surfing areas in the world. It's flawless shape and long right lines have few equals. Rincon has the following ridable points:

First Point

Machine-perfect right lines. Thick and powerful, fast and tubular . . . depending on the tide. Works on any winter swell - a lined-up north is best. Holds shape at any size. During 12 plus surf the problem is getting out. **Caution:** Hazardous rocks along shoreline . . . especially at high tide.

Second Point

The second ridable peak as the wave reaches point and wraps into the cove. Breaks at any size but is best when its big and strong. Rides from here to the beach are more likely at a medium tide. Shallow, unmakeable sections develop at low tide. Not as crowded as First Point.

Third Point/Indicator

The outermost break of Rincon Point. Thick, grinding rights that are rarely makeable. Breaks on any winter swell. Medium tide. Never crowded. **Comment:** Needs size before it works.

La Conchita Beach

Small pop-up beach peaks. Ridable from 1-4 feet. Takes any winter swell. Best shape at medium-high tide. Big swells close out. Sandy beach and bottom.

SOUTHERN CALIFORNIA

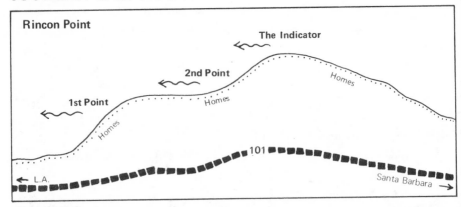

Rincon Point

The Indicator

2nd Point

1st Point

Homes

Homes

Homes

101

L.A.

Santa Barbara

RINCON POINT — 1963. In center is the always crowded "First Point". Barely visible to the extreme right is the tail of a "Second Point" wave as it wraps into the cove. The "Third Point" is even further to the right but out of photo. **Note:** The area between First and Second Point is usually unridable. Occasionally during a large swell and the right tide it becomes makeable. **Also:** The old two-lane road is now a freeway.

The inside section at Rincon readies to throw sometime in the 1960's. **Note:** The island in the background is man-made and is used for oil drilling. The pipeline (top left) can also be seen in photo at bottom of next page.

Long lines at SEACLIFF REEF. ½ mile from shore.

LA CONCHITA POINT has four or five ridable peaks. This is just one of them.

La Conchita Point

Various peaks along a rocky point. Lines peak below the oil pier and peel right for nearly ½ mile. Unmakeable sections separate peaks. Takes any winter swell. Medium-low tide. Ridable from 2 feet up - rarely closes out. **Comment:** Not a Rincon but not as crowded either.

Seacliff Reef

A concentrated peak break nearly ½ mile from shore. Vertical drops with thick rights or lefts. Shoulders quickly flatten as they move into deep water. Breaks on any winter swell. Doesn't show till it's 6 feet or better. Ridable to 20. **Note:** 4 skinny palm trees mark reef's location from freeway. **Comment:** Big waves and long swims - no place for the beginner.

Tropics

Slow-moving rights across an outer reef. Soft and very mushy. Ridable from 2-8 feet - any winter swell. Medium-low tide. **Note:** Camping and facilities available in nearby Hobson Park.

LA CONCHITA POINT. Incoming lines peak below the pier and are makeable for close to 30 yards. Note rocks and boils in foreground.

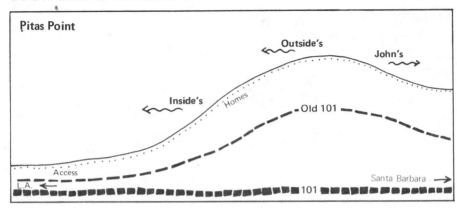

Pitas Point
Outside's
John's
Inside's
Homes
Old 101
Access
L.A. ←
Santa Barbara →
101

PITAS POINT

John's

Summer lefts off the west end of Pitas Point. Ridable from 2-6 feet, south swells. Medium-low tide. Cobblestone bottom and beach. Enter through Faria Park. **Note:** Camping allowed at this rugged beach park.

Outside's

Strong rights breaking off outer point. Well-shaped lineups with some fast, tubular sections. Takes either a north or west swell. Medium-low tide. Ridable from 2-6 feet. **Note:** Beachfront is private - no direct access. Enter from public beaches to the north or south and walk. **Comment:** Well worth the hike.

Insides

Right slides across the inside point. Easy lines that barely break. Works year'round - summer and winter. Kelp keeps it smooth as glass. A 1-5 foot swell and medium tide are usually unbeatable. **Comment:** One of the best learning spots in Santa Barbara county.

PITAS POINT.

A left at "Johns" — PITAS POINT.

The outside lineup — PITAS POINT.

Solimar Reef

A heavy, concentrated peak breaking 300 yards offshore. Steep, vertical drops with a slow right or left line. Needs a 6 foot winter swell and medium-low tide. Never crowded.

Solimar

Punchless, easy breaking rights. Soft lines that peak over an outer reef and crawl toward shore. Many unmakeable sections. Works year'round - summer or winter. Best from 2-6 feet. Medium-low tide.

PITAS POINT. A hollow section looms ahead as rider moves from the "outside" to the "inside" point. Note: Swimmer (foreground) didn't make it.

A winter's day at SOLIMAR. Surf is 4-6 feet, well-shaped, with a slight offshore wind. Those are the Channel Islands in background.

SOUTHERN CALIFORNIA

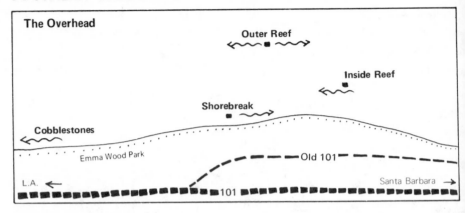

The Overhead

Outer Reef

Inside Reef

Shorebreak

Cobblestones

Emma Wood Park

Old 101

L.A. ←

Santa Barbara →

101

VENTURA OVERHEAD

Outer Peak

Big winter waves. Breaks nearly a ½ mile from shore. Northern lines focus onto a shallow reef creating a steep, concentrated peak. Vertical, top-to-bottom takeoffs followed by a well-shaped right or left shoulder. Rights preferred. Takes any winter swell at any tide. Needs at least 6 feet to break and holds up to 20. **Comment:** A "hairball" peak. Much like Sunset Beach in Hawaii.

Inside Peak

Thick souplines from the outer reef reform and produce strong rights and lefts across the Inside Reef. Takes any winter swell. Ridable from 2-6 feet. Medium-low tide.

Shorebreak

Tubular lefts and right a few yards from shore. Breaks both summer and winter.

Note: During heavy surf a strong rip-current runs to sea (see map). It should be used for easy access to the outer peak. In case of a lost board never attempt swimming against it. You'll only waste your energy and will soon find yourself far out to sea. **Instead** swim into whitewater and let it take you safely to shore. **Also:** Camping is allowed in Emma Woods Park.

Comment: The Overhead is one of the finest big-wave breaks in California. **Remember:** It's powerful and unforgiving and should be ridden by only those experienced in large surf.

Cobblestones

Fast wrapping winter lines. Looks makeable but usually isn't. Breaks on any winter swell. Medium tide. Cobblestones along beach eat up lost boards. **Comment:** Fast and grindy — rarely surfed.

The "outer peak" of the VENTURA OVER-HEAD. It can't get much better!

This surfer didn't know it but he rode this wave into history. This picture was taken at Rincon Point in the early 1960's when surfing was first becoming popular. Crowds were unheard of. You could always get a wave to yourself . . . But now, ten years later things have changed. The crowds are intense. It's common to see 75-150 boards in at one time. Sometimes you can't even park. And that's why this photo has become a classic.

VENTURA OVERHEAD — This is the "Outer Peak" of the Ventura Overhead. It is considered one of the best big-wave reefs along the Southern California coast. It's located a few miles north of Ventura (see map) and almost 1/2 mile from shore. The surfer above has negotiated the takeoff and is lining up the right wall. He could have gone left, but the rights are longer and faster. **Notes:** #1 The main paddling channel is to the extreme left. #2 The wave in foreground wasn't big enough to break at the "outer peak" but will explode at "inside peak".

97

SOUTHERN CALIFORNIA

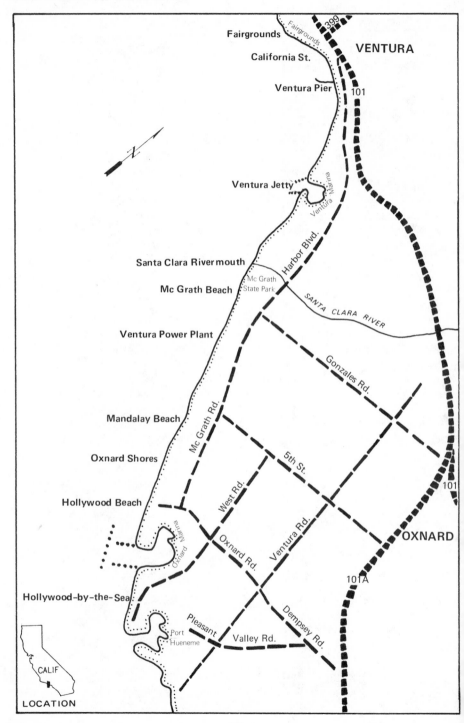

Fairgrounds

Fairgrounds

399

VENTURA

California St.

101

Ventura Pier

Marina

Ventura Jetty

Ventura

Harbor Blvd.

Santa Clara Rivermouth

Mc Grath
State Park

SANTA CLARA RIVER

Mc Grath Beach

Ventura Power Plant

Gonzales Rd.

Mandalay Beach

Oxnard Shores

Mc Grath Rd.

5th St.

101

Hollywood Beach

West Rd.

OXNARD

Oxnard Marina

Oxnard Rd.

Ventura Rd.

Hollywood-by-the-Sea

101A

Port
Hueneme

Pleasant

Dempsey Rd.

Valley Rd.

CALIF

LOCATION

Two-up at FAIRGROUNDS . . . one is turning back, the other is "goin for it". Swimmer (foreground) tried and failed.

VENTURA POINT

Fairgrounds

Powerful, right lines off the outermost point. Ridable from 2-8 feet. Any winter swell. Medium-low tide. Unmakeable sections loom as line wraps toward the inside point. **Comment:** A speed wave . . . little time for anything fancy. The "juice" break of Ventura Point.

California Street

Insides: Smooth, well-shaped rights off the inside point. Breaks both summer and winter. Ridable from 2-6 feet. Best on a lined-up north or west swell. Medium-low tide. **Comment:** Easy peaks everywhere . . . breaks like Waikiki, Hawaii. An excellent beginners spot when it's small.

Outside's: Takes over as surf nears 8 feet. Big, thick lines that feather on an outer reef and peel right along a deep channel. Ridable from 8-20 feet. Any winter swell any tide. **Caution:** Strong shoreline currents during heavy surf. **Comment:** A powerful break . . . experienced, big-wave riders only.

A big day at the VENTURA PIER.

Shapely ladies.

VENTURA POINT during a huge west swell. To the extreme right is "Fairgrounds" which has closed out. In the middle is the normal lineup for "California Street". It looks ridable but isn't. Too many sections. To the extreme left (not shown) is the outside peak of California Street. This is the spot to ride.

The VENTURA PIER (south side). Pictured is what can result when Mother Nature blends the right ingredients of wind, swell, and tide.

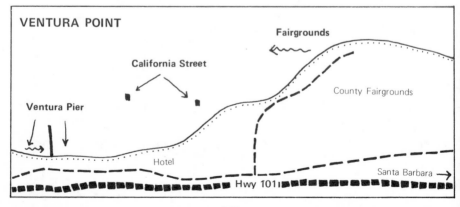

VENTURA POINT

Fairgrounds

California Street

Ventura Pier

County Fairgrounds

Hotel

Hwy 101

Santa Barbara →

VENTURA PIER

SANTA CLARA RIVERMOUTH.

VENTURA JETTY.

MANDALAY BEACH.

Ventura Pier
Sandbar peaks - south side of pier. Well-shaped lefts and some rights. Breaks from 2-6 feet north/west swell. Medium-low tide. **Comment:** A tempermental peak . . . but perfect when it works.

Ventura Jetty
Small, well-shaped lefts into main channel. Needs a huge winter swell - and low tide. Ridable from 1-5 feet. **Comment:** Break is protected from large swells, few hazards. A good spot for beginners.

Santa Clara Rivermouth
Powerful peaks and lines. Breaks ¼ mile offshore. Ridable from 2-5 feet. Any swell. Large waves hold shape but getting out is nearly impossible. Shape best after heavy winter rains. **Comment:** A spooky break . . . similar to the Sloughs in San Diego.

McGrath Beach
3 miles of shifting beach peaks. Takes any swell, any tide. Best from 2-5 feet above that and it gets pretty hairy. **Note:** Camping allowed at this beautiful seaside park.

Ventura Power Plant
Beach surf similar to that of McGrath. Warm water emitted by steam plant. Ridable from 2-5 feet. Any swell, any tide. **Comment:** An isolated spot - rarely surfed.

Mandalay Beach/Oxnard Shores
Typical beach surf . . . pop-up peaks with short right and left lines. Breaks on any swell from 2-6 feet. Medium tide. Blows out on the slightest of winds. **Note:** The constant scene of heavy damage caused by big winter surf.

Hollywood Beach
Beach peaks. North of entrance to Mandalay Bay. Best in winter on any 2-6 foot swell. Medium tide. Sandy beach and bottom. Stays glassy until late mornings. Never crowded.

A clean north swell peels into HOLLYWOOD-by-the-SEA. In background is the outer break-wall at the entrance to Mandalay Bay.

After successfully negotiating an almost vertical takeoff, this surfer is looking into the eye of a gnarly, HOLLYWOOD wall. Note concave shape of the wave's face. It's already beginning to suck!

HOLLYWOOD-BY-THE-SEA

One of the best beach breaks in all of California. A mile of perfection peaks. Tube rights and lefts. Super steep take-offs with hollow lines to follow. Takes any winter swell from 2-15 feet. Medium tide best. Surf is always 2-3 feet bigger than anywhere else. **Note:** Large swells hold shape but getting outside becomes extremely difficult - no channels. **Caution:** Take heed . . . unfriendly locals rip off unattended autos. **Comment:** A classic winter spot. Pumps with the juice of an Hawaiian wave.

What else can be said except . . . "another HOLLYWOOD dazzler".

HOLLYWOOD breaks top-to-bottom. Turning at the top is not advised.

VENTURA PIER. A late afternoon on the south side.

SOUTHERN CALIFORNIA

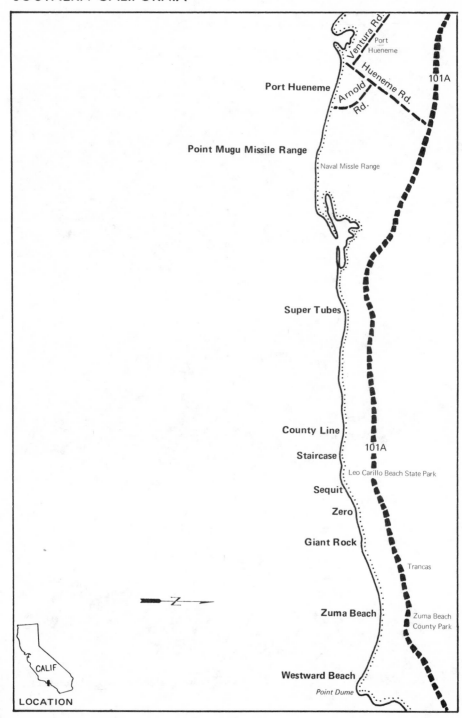

Port Hueneme

Point Mugu Missile Range

Super Tubes

County Line

Staircase

Sequit

Zero

Giant Rock

Zuma Beach

Westward Beach

Point Dume

Ventura Rd.

Port Hueneme

Hueneme Rd.

Arnold Rd.

101A

Naval Missle Range

101A

Leo Carillo Beach State Park

Trancas

Zuma Beach County Park

CALIF

LOCATION

SUPER TUBES breaks just like the "Pipeline" of Hawaii except its a right and its in California.

PORT HUENEME. Pictured above is the northern boundary of the Point Mugu Missile Range. This is the last accessible spot until "Super Tubes".

Port Hueneme

Miles of uncrowded beach surf. Sandbar peaks ridable from 2-5 feet. Takes any swell but best in winter. Shape is unpredictable - best when off shores blow out of valley. **Note:** Located 5 miles off the main highway. Rarely ridden by anyone except area locals.

Point Mugu Missle Range

All kinds of point and beach surf along 3 miles of government property. Consistent surf all year but access is heavily restricted. **Comment:** Very little is known of area and likely will remain that way.

Super Tubes

A super-hot point break. Clean west swells produce fast zippers that break right in front of a huge seawall. Peaks first explode over a clump of rocks - then peel and spit for shore. Tide very critical . . . medium-low a must. **Caution:** Super dangerous if conditions aren't together.

SOUTHERN CALIFORNIA

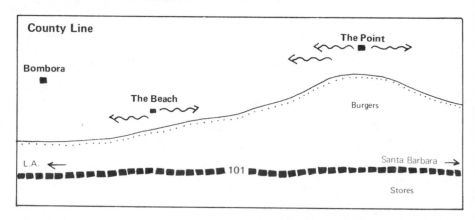

COUNTY LINE

The Point
Clean, pop-up peaks off the northern point. Mostly rights and some lefts. Breaks all year but shape is usually better in winter. Ridable from 2-10 ft. Any tide but medium-low is preferred.

The Beach
Smooth beach surf - ½ mile south of point. Outer reefs produce consistent peaks with slow, two-way shoulders. Breaks from 2-10 feet on any swell. Big west swells are best. Medium tide. Sand bottom and beach. **Caution:** Violent rip currents during heavy surf. **Comment:** A safe place to surf if swell is under 4 feet.

Bombora
Huge peaks breaking ¼ mile from shore. Vertical takeoffs that quckly flatten into deep, murky water. Needs a 10 foot swell to break. **Note:** Last surfed in 1953. **Comment:** A big drop . . . nothing else. Not worth the risk.

Lines stack up at SUPER TUBES.

Above: GIANT ROCK.
Below: "The Beach" of COUNTY LINE.

SEQUIT — During average surf (1-4 feet), the normal lineup is slightly to the left of the large rock. During heavier surf (5 feet +), the takeoff point moves about 25 yards south onto another reef. **Note:** Because of large crowds, the outer point (upper center) is now being ridden.

Staircase
Thick, shifting peaks a mile north of Sequit. Mellow and uncrowded. Ridable from 2-8 feet - any swell. Breaks year'-round. Medium tide best. **Note:** Private beach front . . . Look for dirt trail that leads to the sea.

Sequit
An all year reef break. Swells peak near a large rock and peel right for 150 yards. Takes any swell but favors a south. Ridable 2-8 feet. Medium-low tide. Thick kelp helps keep the chop down. Water is usually 5° colder than rest of coast. Camping allowed in state park across highway. **Note:** The far northern point is now being surfed. But only when conditions are perfect.

Zero
Long, uncrowded lefts off a submerged point. Vertical drops with piping left tubes. Ends in a backbreaking shorebreak. Takes any swell but is primo during a strong south. Ridable from 3-15 feet. Medium-low tide. Closes out when tide is high. **Note:** Area is privately own and direct access restricted. Enter from Sequit and walk south. **Caution:** Strong rip currents during heavy surf. Never surf alone.

Giant Rock
A fast right. Peaks next to a large rock and peels toward shore. Ridable from 1-4 feet. Larger swells close out. Takes any swell but a south is best. Medium-low tide preferred. **Note:** Although privately owned, L. A. County has provided a path for public access. **Caution:** Stay below mean high tide line - property owners get uptight.

Zuma Beach
Miles of uncrowded beach break. Shifty peaks . . . right and left. Ridable on any swell from 1-5 feet. Medium-high tide. Unridable during heavy surf. Conditions are usually perfect when offshores roar out of the mountain canyons. Then its steep and super hollow. **Note:** Shape is very unpredictable. Depends on the contour of the shifting sand bottom.

Westward Beach
Steep, tubular beach peaks. ½ mile south of Zuma. Breaks on any swell from 2-10 feet. Medium tide. **Comment:** Starts to vibrate during heavy south swells. Hollow lefts up and down beach. Resembles "Pipeline" but steeper. Boards have a hard time getting out. Bodysurfers take over and rip. **Caution:** This is one of the strongest beach breaks in Southern California. No place for the inexperienced.

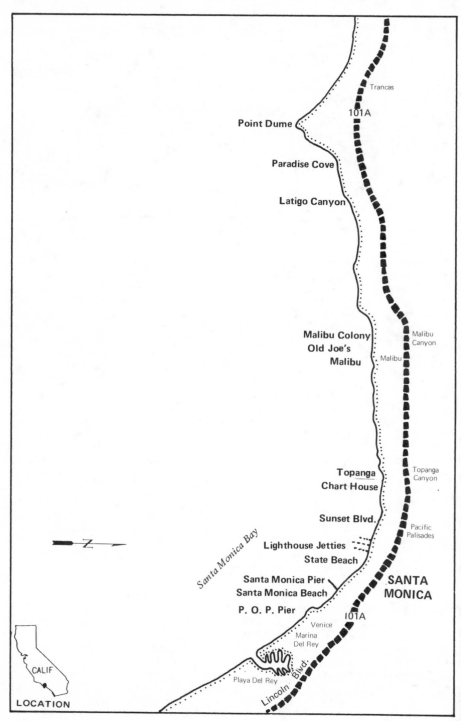

Trancas

101A

Point Dume

Paradise Cove

Latigo Canyon

Malibu Colony
Old Joe's
Malibu

Malibu
Canyon

Malibu

Topanga
Chart House

Topanga
Canyon

Sunset Blvd.

Pacific
Palisades

Lighthouse Jetties

State Beach

Santa Monica Pier
Santa Monica Beach

SANTA
MONICA

P. O. P. Pier

101A

Santa Monica Bay

Venice

Marina
Del Rey

Lincoln Blvd.

Playa Del Rey

N

CALIF

LOCATION

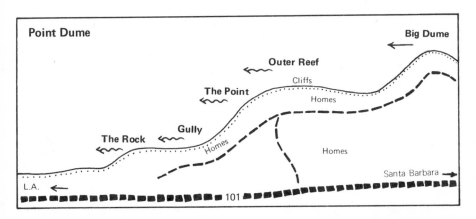

POINT DUME
A private point break. Limited to members and guests only. Ridable all year on both summer and winter swells. Closest public access is Paradise Cove to south or Westward Beach to north. Steep cliffs and barbed wire fences prevent direct access. Members resent outsiders - keep below high tide line. The following spots are surfed:

Big Dume
Thick, hairy rights off the far northern point. Needs a huge south or west swell. 8 feet or better. Medium-low tide. **Comment:** Rarely surfed.

Outer Reef
A small reef in front of the inside point. Peaks right or left. Rights are long but somewhat slow. The lefts are short and very quick. Breaks on any swell. Medium tide. **Caution:** Watch for jagged rocks close to shore.

The Point
Another small peak. 100 yds. below Outer Reef. Fast right tubes. Many sections and bowls. Breaks from 2-6 feet. Winter swells. Needs high tide. **Note:** During large swells rides from Outer's to The Point are possible.

The Gully
Small peaks - left and right. Ridable when surf is below 4 feet. Medium tide. **Comment:** Few hazards - a good place to learn.

POINT DUME — Good size but still slow and mushy.

A longboarder eases below a glossy slider at the MALIBU COLONY.

Paradise Cove
Once in a lifetime lefts. Breaks along beach south of pier. Usually just shorebreak. Area is privately owned and surfing not allowed. **Comment:** Don't bother.

SOUTHERN CALIFORNIA

Latigo Canyon
Inconsistent summer surf. Slow mushy rights off a rocky point. Breaks from 2-6 feet. Needs a strong south swell. Low tide. **Note:** Beach is private - direct access prohibited. Enter from public beach ¼ mile south. **Comment:** Never crowded . . . Lazy summer surf.

Malibu Colony
A Malibu exclusive. Private surfing for the members of this classy beachfront community. Takes any swell. But a south or west are always best. Thick peaks with soft, mushy lineups. Needs low tide to work. Sandy beach and bottom. **Note:** No direct access. Requires a 2 mile hike from Surfrider Beach or . . .

Old Joe's
Quick lefts. Breaks off a small point-like reef north of the Malibu Lagoon. Needs a 2-8 foot south swell. Medium tide preferred. **Comment:** Shape is very tempermental - can change in a matter of minutes.

A south swell peels into LATIGO.

A classic turn at the COLONY.

MALIBU.

TOPANGA.

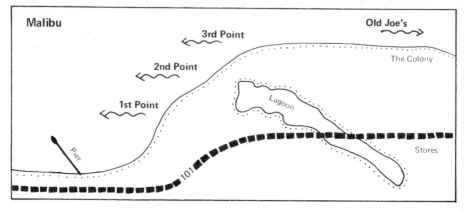

MALIBU POINT

First Point

One of the most perfect summer breaks in all of California. Pure rights off a rocky point. Breaks on a south or southwest swell. Winter surf has no effect. Normal size is between 2-4 feet. Stronger swells can sometimes produce 6-8 foot surf. Shape is outstanding - at any tide. Becomes very hollow as tide drops. At high tide it's a bit slow. Rarely blows out except during a south wind. Normal sea breezes are almost offshore. **Comment:** Summer perfection . . . if you can take the crowds.

Second Point

Bigger and faster rights . . . but not as long. Never as crowded as the main point. Needs an incoming medium tide. Unmakeable at low. **Comment:** Steep takeoffs with a hollow, peeling tube. Line dies in a small, sand-bottom lagoon.

Third Point

Fast, smoking rights off the far northern point. Zipper tubes that are rarely makeable. Ridable from 3-6 feet. Large swells break from the Third to the Second Point. Medium tide a must. **Comment:** Away from the jamming Malibu crowd.

The MALIBU lineup. The famous "first point" is to the left of the flagpole. The "second point" is visible to the right of the guard tower. The third point (not shown) is to the extreme right. Note: The first point is very crowded while the second point is nearly empty.

"Da Cat" . . . Malibu, 1964. There is no question that Mickey Dora will go down in surfing history as the man who rode Malibu better than anyone ever has or probably ever will.

In 1965 Johnny Fain and Mickey Dora battled it out in one of the preliminary heats of the Malibu Contest. Both repeatedly ripped the small but super-shaped tubes. Then as fate had it, they met on the same wave and the rest is history . . . #1 Fain takes off and prepares for a high-scoring ride. #2 Fain is trimmed and scoring lots of points. Little does he know that Da Cat is moving in for the kill. #3 Mickey easily dusts off Fain and then rides **backwards** across the inside section. #4 Fain frantically chases a smiling Mickey Dora. **Note:** Neither won the heat, but both provided surfing with a moment that will never be forgotten.

SANTA MONICA PIER. Surf like this can usually be found during summer months when the warm Santa Ana winds blow in from the desert.

The fast lines of CHART HOUSE.

Winter lines wrap onto the point where SUNSET BLVD. meets the Pacific Ocean.

Topanga

A long right point break. Takes any swell but shape is best on a strong west. Ridable from 2-10 feet. Medium-low tide. Many sections between point and main beach . . . rarely makeable. Rocky bottom - sandy beach. Few hazards. A safe place to surf.

Chart House

Gnarly rights breaking below Steak House. Suckular tubes that spit and grind. Needs a 2-8 foot south or west swell. Low tide a must! **Caution:** Strong shoreline currents and protruding rocks — a hairball spot.

Sunset Blvd.

A long point break. Peels right from Sunset Blvd. to the Bel-Air Bay Club. Easy peak takeoffs with mild right lines. Sections and flat spots - depending on tide. Medium-low tide preferred. Breaks on any swell from 3-10 feet. Shape is usually better n winter. **Comment:** A super beginners break with lots of room for everyone.

SOUTHERN CALIFORNIA

Winter lines get worked over at one of the LIGHTHOUSE JETTIES.

A LIGHTHOUSE smoker north of Tower 14.

Small juice at the SANTA MONICA PIER.

Lighthouse Jetties

Little right shooters off the Santa Monica beach jetties. Steep takeoffs with quickzip tubes. Works on any swell from 1-4 feet. Medium-low tide. Sandy beach and bottom. **Comment:** Unridable during heavy surf.

State Beach

Two-way beach peaks. Breaks on any swell from 2-8 feet. Medium tide. During heavy surf lines peak on an outer reef and peel left till they end in a pounding shorebreak. Rock and sand bottom. Sandy beach. **Note:** Excellent bodysurfing during the large summer swells. **Comment:** A very popular beach break for Santa Monica locals.

Santa Monica Pier

Unpredictable beach peaks on both sides of pier. Breaks on any swell - summer or winter. Shape is usually best during a peaky west swell. Ridable from 1-5 feet. Medium tide. Sandy beach and bottom.

Santa Monica Beach

Two long miles of unpredictable beach surf. Breaks on any swell - summer or winter. Ridable from 1-5 feet with a medium tide. Lots of room . . . never too crowded. **Note:** Best during a small peaky west swell. **Comment:** A typical beach break - hit or miss.

A clean west swell at STATE BEACH. The surf is not quite large enough to break on the outer sandbar.

TOPANGA CANYON — As good as it gets. Photo was taken during a 3-5 foot west swell with a medium tide.

P. O. P. Pier

Nothing works here except the surf. The pier is closed - awaiting its fate. But during strong swells lines peak off north side of pier and grind left. Takes any swell but favors a strong south. Medium-low tide. **Caution:** Waves break in front of pilings - lower tides a must. **Note:** Pier may soon be destroyed and with it . . . the gnarly P.O.P. lefts.

The gnarly shorebreak of P.O.P. PIER.

SOUTHERN CALIFORNIA

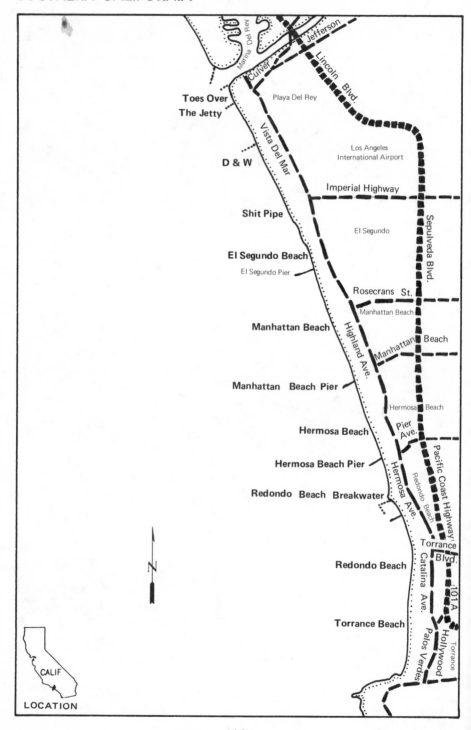

Marina Del Rey

Jefferson

Culver

Lincoln Blvd.

Toes Over
The Jetty

Playa Del Rey

Vista Del Mar

D & W

Los Angeles
International Airport

Imperial Highway

Shit Pipe

El Segundo

Sepulveda Blvd.

El Segundo Beach

El Segundo Pier

Rosecrans St.

Manhattan Beach

Manhattan Beach

Highland Ave.

Manhattan Beach

Manhattan Beach Pier

Hermosa Beach

Hermosa Beach

Pier Ave.

Hermosa Beach Pier

Hermosa Ave.

Redondo Beach Breakwater

Redondo Beach

Pacific Coast Highway

Torrance Blvd.

101A

Redondo Beach

Catalina Ave.

Hollywood

Torrance

Palos Verdes

Torrance Beach

N

CALIF

LOCATION

The beach surf of Playa Del Rey. In background is the outer seawall of Marina Del Rey harbor.

Winter lines roar into the REDONDO BEACH BREAKWATER.

Toes Over
Small but tubular rights off the south jetty of Ballona Creek. Breaks on any swell. Best on a 2-5 foot south. Medium tide. **Comment:** Shape is very unpredictable . . . A "sometimes" spot even for the locals of Playa Del Rey.

The Jetty
Well-shaped lefts off the end of a small jetty. Ridable on most swells from 2-5 feet. Medium-low tide. Bigger swells line up and close out. **Note:** Favors a 2-5 foot south swell.

D & W
Long rights off jetty. Breaks year'round. Best on a 2-6 foot north swell. Medium tide. Usually steep with a fast inside line up. Unmakeable at low tide. **Also:** Good beach surf south of jetty break. Easy right and left peaks. Sandy beach and bottom. Few hazards - easy access. **Comment:** A safe place for beginners.

Shit Pipe
Shouldering lefts breaking next to an underwater sewage pipe. Needs a 3-8 north/west swell. Incoming tide. Best in early mornings before the onshore winds blow. **Comment:** An erratic surf break . . . dangerous if all conditions are not working.

SOUTHERN CALIFORNIA

A foamy, backside slider — 200 yards north of the HERMOSA BEACH PIER.

HERMOSA BEACH — Rider stares ahead as a healthy section begins to ripple.

A beach wave unloads onto a shallow sandbar and grinds toward deep water.

El Segundo

Beach: Thick peaks along a mile of sandy beach. Breaks year'round. Best in winter on a peaky north or west swell. Medium tide. Strong south swells usually close out. Never crowded. **Note:** Nearest legal parking - ½ mile south in Manhattan Beach.

Pier: Beach peaks - north side. Breaks on any swell from 1-8 feet. Any tide. Thick walls with occasional fast inside line ups. Sandy beach and bottom. **Comment:** Peaks are usually well-shaped.

MANHATTAN BEACH. Top turning an old tattooed longboard.

Foreground: A small TORRANCE BEACH peeler. Background: The cliffs of the Palos Verdes Peninsula.

Manhattan Beach Pier

Steep hardbreaking peaks on both sides of pier. Swells focus onto sandbars and peel right or left. Takes any swell but best on 3-6 foot peaky north.

Strong lines close out. Shape depends on contour of the shifting sand bottom. Medium-high tide helps. **Comment:** Good bodysurfing during summer months . . . after the boards have left.

Manhattan/Hermosa Beach

5 miles of beach surf. Ridable year'-round on any swell. Best on a peaky 2-6 foot winter swell. Medium tide. Waves over 6 feet usually close out. Shape varys radically — depends on contour of sand bottom. Lots of room for surfers, matters, knee boarders, bodysurfers etc. . . **Comment:** Always has some kind of ridable surf.

SOUTHERN CALIFORNIA

Hermosa Beach Pier
Sandbar peaks - both sides of pier. Breaks on any swell. Best on a 2-6 foot north or west. Medium tide. Strong lines usually close out.

Redondo Beach Breakwater
A powerful winter break. Northern lines focus onto outside reef developing into steep, shifting peaks with grinding left walls. Ends in murderous shorepound. Requires at least a 6-15 foot swell. Medium-low tide. Smaller surf is typical beach break - ¼ mile north of jetty. **Comment:** Small surf is routine . . . needs size before it cooks.

Redondo/Torrance Beach
Miles of typical beach surf. Shifty peaks with two way lines. Ridable all year. Shape best during 2-6 foot peaky west swells. Medium tide preferred. Rarely ridable above 6 feet. Sandy bottom cannot hold size. **Note:** Palos Verdes and Catalina deflect south swells. North and west swells hit full on.

A small rider slides across a Breakwater wall.

Winter lines explode at D&W. Rock jetty is to the right of photo.

REDONDO BEACH BREAKWATER — Small surf at the Breakwater has mediocre shape and big crowds. It's during the big winter swells that it reaches full potential — thick concentrated peaks with long left walls (see above). Compare this photo with the one at bottom of next page and note how size affects the crowd.

"stretchin for five" . . . across a clean peak at Hermosa Beach. Note: Photo was taken in late 1960's.

A crowded day at the REDONDO BEACH BREAKWATER. When the surf gets big most of the crowd moves to the beach.

SOUTHERN CALIFORNIA

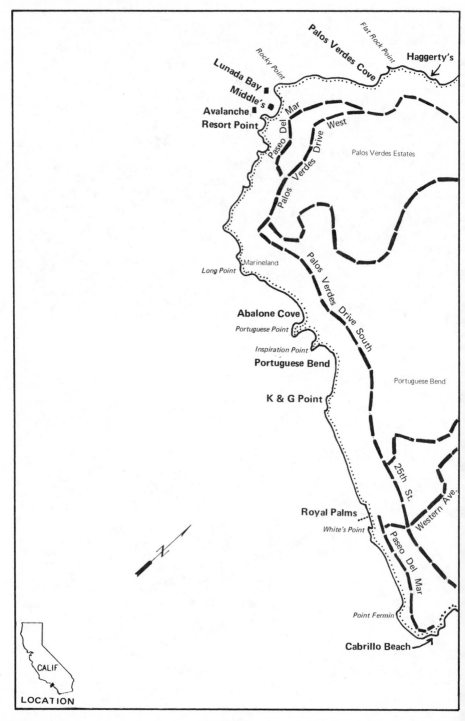

Palos Verdes Cove

Flat Rock Point

Haggerty's

Rocky Point

Lunada Bay

Middle's

Avalanche

Resort Point

Paseo Del Mar

Palos Verdes Drive West

Palos Verdes Estates

Marineland

Long Point

Abalone Cove

Portuguese Point

Inspiration Point

Portuguese Bend

Palos Verdes Drive South

Portuguese Bend

K & G Point

25th St.

Western Ave.

Royal Palms

White's Point

Paseo Del Mar

Point Fermin

Cabrillo Beach

N

CALIF

LOCATION

Haggerty's

Thick winter lefts. Peak takeoffs with long, mellow lines. Breaks best on a north swell from 5-15 feet. Favors medium tide. Smaller rights and lefts break on reef 150 yds. inside main peak. Steep cliffs and lots of rocks. **Comment:** A primo winter break - but only when it's big and lined up.

PALOS VERDES COVE

One of the spots where California surfing got its start . . . a way back. It's mainly a winter break that needs a big strong north swell. 4 reefs can be ridden:

Ski Jump

A big, slow, mushy right. Needs at least a 10 foot swell before it breaks. Peaks in front of Flatrock Point. **Comment:** Rarely breaks and rarely ridden.

North Reef

The only juice of The Cove. Fast rights and lefts. Sometimes tubular depending on tide. Ridable from 2-5 feet. Medium-high tide. **Caution:** Watch for rocks and holes at low tide.

The Channel

The main break. Slow rolling right and left walls. Rights preferred! Works from 3-10 feet any strong winter swell. Medium-low tide. **Note:** Summer swells sometimes generate good beginners surf.

The Indicator

Hairy lefts off the southern point. Thick walls that peak and push left for nearly 100 yards. Breaks from 6 feet and up. Medium tide. Sheer cliffs and boulders along shoreline. **Note:** Signals approaching set for The Cove.

A lone line peels at HAGGERTY's (middle of photo). Below: The surf of Torrance Beach.

The Palos Verdes Cove . . . Top: "the indicator". Bottom: "the channel".

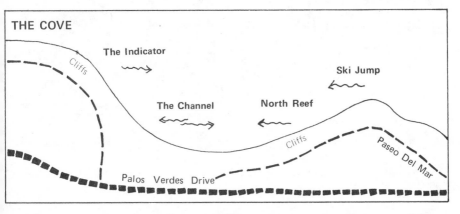

THE COVE

The Indicator

Cliffs

Ski Jump

The Channel

North Reef

Cliffs

Paseo Del Mar

Palos Verdes Drive

SOUTHERN CALIFORNIA

Someone yelled . . . "outside" . . . and everyone scratched for the horizon. Location: The Palos Verdes Cove . . . a long time ago.

Off and tracking at the Palos Verdes "Indicator". Although large, these waves are usually slow and mushy.

Everyone is paddling for the outside as a three wave set rolls into HAGGERTY'S. It's wintertime. The swell is from the northwest 6-8 feet. The tide is medium. Everything is working — Haggerty's is at its best.

LUNADA BAY around 1953. Alot has changed since this photo was taken. The once rolling farmlands of Palos Verdes have been sold, resold, and sold again. Houses, apartments, and condominiums have been built. Thousands of people have moved in. Shopping centers and burger stands are everywhere . . . But out there — in the water, nothing has changed. Every winter huge northern walls still explode off the far point. Lunada Bay still produces some of the best big-wave surf in California.

The lineup at LUNADA BAY. 10 foot lines are pumping onto the north point. Surfer (center) has positioned perfectly and is about to drop. Note: Approaching set could cause surfer (lower left) some trouble.

Lunada Bay

Massive winter walls. Steep peaks exploding over a shallow rock reef. Gnarly rights that grind in front of a rock ledge and then flatten as they enter deep water. Needs at least an 8 foot swell before it works. Ridable to 20, Medium tide the safest. Steep cliffs and rocks along shoreline. **Caution:** Big waves only. Not for the inexperienced or beginning surfer.

Middle's

A reef located in the middle of Lunada Bay. Rights and lefts. Ridable from 1-4 feet - any winter swell. Medium tide. **Caution:** Exposed rocks at low tide. **Comment:** Mild beach-type surf. Few hazards. Good for beginners.

Avalanche

A big hairball peak and nothing else. Breaks on a small pile of rocks and immediately backs off in deep water. **Comment:** A risky spot - rarely worth the paddle.

Resort Point

Dangerous, seldom ridden rights. Breaks on a jagged shelf with large body-sized holes. Pumps and grinds. Takes a 3-8 foot north swell. Medium tide. **Note:** Conditions very dangerous . . . rarely ridden.

SOUTHERN CALIFORNIA

Abalone Cove
A private beach with uncrowded winter waves. Lefts off the south point of cove. Needs a 4-10 foot west swell. Low tide. **Note:** Private property - access limited to a privileged few.

Portuguese Bend
Pier, beach, and seawall generate good year'round surf. Takes any swell. Ridable from 2-6 feet. Medium-high tide. Shape varys according to sand bottom. **Note:** A private beach club . . . access restricted to members and guests only.

K & G Point
Large lefts off a ledgy point. 6 feet plus before it breaks. South swell. Medium-low tide the safest. A hazardous rock beach. **Comment:** Area is private, access restricted . . . rarely worth the hassle.

Ground level at the P.V. COVE.

Gnarlburgers at LUNADA BAY.

Private surf of PORTUGUESE BEND.

A place called "Middles" — LUNADA BAY.

A late evening line . . . about to peel.

A "Jetty" left at ROYAL PALMS.

CABRILLO BEACH as never seen before.

Royal Palms

A favorite break for the locals of San Pedro. Has surf in two spots:

The Point: A mellow right off a rock point. Slow lineups with lots of maneuvering room. Hot sections at low tide. Best on a 3-8 foot winter swell. Favors medium-low tide.

The Jetty: Short but well-shaped lefts. Breaks off north side of rock seawall. Ridable from 1-5 feet on any swell. Shapes best at medium-low tide.

Cabrillo Beach

Year'round beach peaks. Winter swells are thick and hard breaking. Summer surf is soft and mushy. Shape best at medium-high tide. Sandy bottom and beach. **Comment:** Few hazards . . . an excellent place for beginners.

What its like to be "caught inside" at LUNADA BAY.

One of the few "secret spots" left in Southern California.

SOUTHERN CALIFORNIA

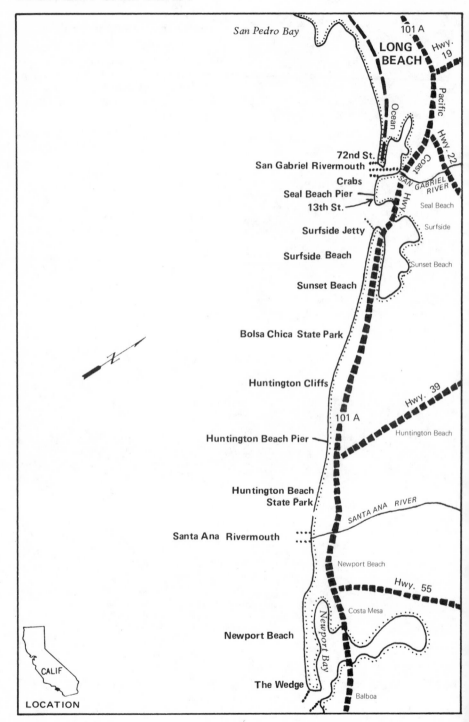

SAN GABRIEL RIVERMOUTH.

The jetty at CRABS in Seal Beach.

Pictured here is better than average surf for SEAL BEACH. The swell is from the west, 3-4 feet. The tide: medium-low. Photo was taken 30 feet south of the pier.

72nd Street
Inconsistent left slides off the north jetty. Needs a healthy 3-8 foot southwest swell before it will break. Medium-low tide. **Comment:** Size and shape are unpredictable_____ usually bumpy and blown out.

San Gabriel Rivermouth/Power Plant
The power plant is gone but the waves aren't. Soft sandbar peaks between jetties. Best on a 2-6 foot south or west swell. Low tide. Usually glassy. 70° water all year. **Note:** Warm water attracts rays and small sandsharks . . . step lightly. **Comment:** An excellent beginners break. Safe and easy to ride.

Crabs
Right slides off a small rock jetty. Just south of the rivermouth. Breaks from 2-5 feet. South or west swell. Medium-low tide. Sandy beach and bottom. **Comment:** A good beginners spot.

Seal Beach Pier
Beach peaks - both sides of pier. Usually fast and hard'breaking. Best on a 2-5 foot west swell. Medium-low tide. Stronger swells tend to line up and close out. Sandy beach and bottom. **Comment:** Shape will vary according to shifting sand bottom.

13th Sreet
An unpredictable winter peak. Doesn't break very often. When it does . . . it's a smoker. Needs a strong (3-10 foot) winter swell and low tide. Shape depends on contour of sand bottom. **Caution:** Watch for strong currents and shorebreak during heavy surf.

SOUTHERN CALIFORNIA

An unusual day at the HUNTINGTON CLIFFS. A large, well-shaped west swell is sweeping into Huntington Beach. Air temperature: 75°. Visibility: 30 miles. The city of San Pedro is visible in background.

Surfside Jetty
Right lines south of harbor seawall. Thick peak takeoffs with powerful, well-shaped walls. Ends in a shattering shorebreak. Starts to break at 6 feet and can reach 20. Takes any winter swell. Low tide. Shape depends on shifting sand bottom. **Note:** Area is a colony of private beach homes. Enter from Sunset Beach - a mile south.

HUNTINGTON BEACH PIER — north side.

Surfside/Sunset Beach
Two miles of uncrowded beach peaks. Breaks on any swell from 2-6 feet. Shape usually best at medium-high tide but depends on contour of bottom. **Comment:** Dependable sandbar peaks and hardly ever crowded.

Bolsa Chica State Park
Another 3 miles of easybreaking beach waves. Ridable on any swell from 1-6 feet. Hard to get out during heavy surf. Medium-low tide will give it some punch. **Note:** Blown out quickly by northwest winds . . . early mornings are best.

The 13th Street of Seal Beach . . . A small but shapely peak.

Every summer, Huntington Beach holds an annual surfing contest. If you win you're "top dog" for the year. But to win you must outperform hundreds of name surfers from around the world. You must "go for it" — all out all the time . . . And that's what this rider is doing as he heads into the pier. A mistake in here could mean "curtains".

The outer sandbar • HUNTINGTON CLIFFS.

Clean winter lines unwind into HUNTINGTON CLIFFS. Catalina Island is in background.

Huntington Cliffs
Easy peaks with mellow lines - 1/4 mile offshore. Usually mushy and powerless. Takes any swell. Ridable from 3-10 feet. Medium-low tide. The larger winter swells are sometimes very well-shaped. **Comment:** Lots of room and plenty of surf. A safe place.

Huntington Beach Pier
Consistent sandbar peaks on both sides of pier. Winter rights on north. Summer lefts on south. Ridable from 2-8 feet - any swell. Usually best at medium tide. Shape depends on contour of sand bottom. **Note:** Annual mob scene of the Huntington Beach Surfing Contest — held in September (waves permitting).

Huntington Beach State Park
Peak surf along 2 miles of wide sandy beach. Easy takeoffs with mild rights and lefts. Can break hard at times. Takes any swell from 2-10 feet. Medium-low tide. **Comment:** Breaks the same as rest of Huntington but not as crowded.

131

SOUTHERN CALIFORNIA

Santa Ana Rivermouth
Consistent year'round peaks. Speed and shape of wave depends on the contour of sandbars which form at the rivermouth. Ridable from 2-6 feet. Medium-low tide. Larger surf tends to close out. **Caution:** Dangerous current during times of heavy surf . . . use extreme caution. **Comment:** Spot always seems to have some kind of ridable surf.

The south end of the SANTA ANA RIVERMOUTH.

Newport Beach
Typical beach surf along 2 miles of crowded coastline. Ridable year round from 2-6 feet. Medium-low tide. Heavy surf closes out. Shape varys according to the shifting sand bottom. **Comment:** Some swells produce better surf in one place than another. Check the whole area and pick the peak that's working best.

The Wedge
Hydraulic body explosions. A wedge-shaped peak formed when incoming swell meets outgoing backwash. Must have a south swell and medium tide. Starts breaking at 2 feet but best from 5 on up. **Note:** A very popular bodysurfing beach - no surfboards allowed. **Caution:** Strong surf breakng in shallow water . . . a dangerous combination. For experienced bodysurfers only!

Two-way peaks along NEWPORT BEACH.

SANTA ANA RIVERMOUTH. Low tide lines grind in front of a large winter sandbar.

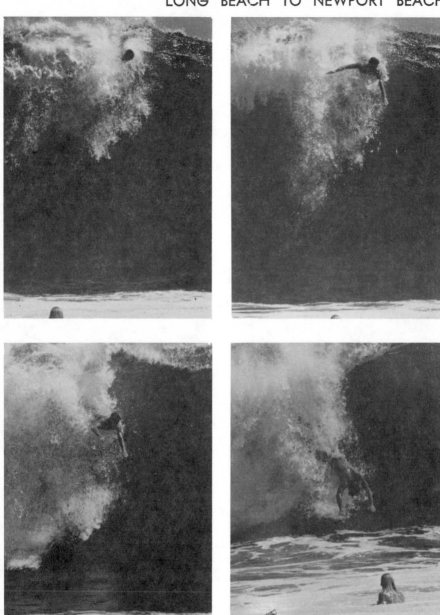

The NEWPORT WEDGE is considered one of the most dangerous body-surfing breaks in all of California. This sequence will prove why . . . #1 — Swimmer has made the takeoff and is hanging in the lip as the wave begins to hollow out. #2 — He has taken the drop position and is glancing left as he lines up the shoulder. In #3 he is sliding down the face while above the crest readies to dump. #4 — The entire wave is about to explode and there's no place to go but straight down. This moment is critical. A mistake could mean a broken neck. But no fear, this bodysurfer is about to dive **down** and **back through** the wave to safety. **Note:** Swimmer at the bottom of #4 is sitting in only 2-3 feet of water.

SOUTHERN CALIFORNIA

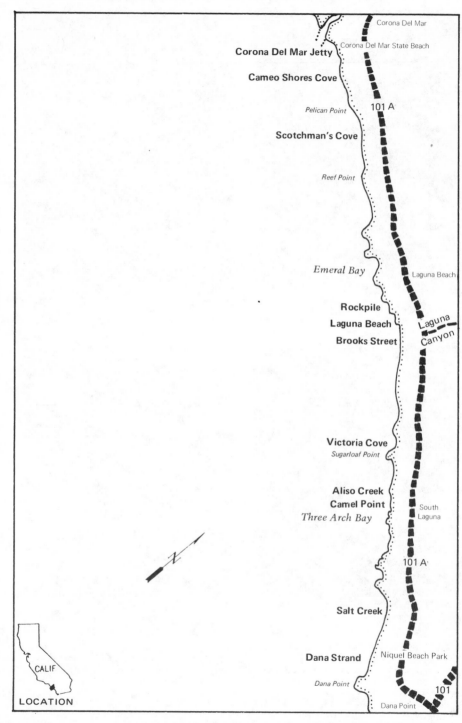

Corona Del Mar

Corona Del Mar Jetty

Corona Del Mar State Beach

Cameo Shores Cove

101 A

Pelican Point

Scotchman's Cove

Reef Point

Emeral Bay

Laguna Beach

Rockpile

Laguna Beach

Laguna

Brooks Street

Canyon

Victoria Cove

Sugarloaf Point

Aliso Creek

Camel Point

South
Laguna

Three Arch Bay

101 A

Salt Creek

Dana Strand

Niquel Beach Park

Dana Point

101

CALIF

LOCATION

Dana Point

⌐A 6 foot summer swell pumps onto a shallow reef in Laguna Beach. Note the unusual absence of surfers and swimmers.

SCOTCHMAN'S COVE.

Corona Del Mar Jetty
Long summer rights breaking off the south seawell of Newport Harbor. Sometimes fast and well-shaped. Takes a 3-8 foot south swell and high tide. Prevailing winds are usually offshore. Sandy bottom and beach. **Caution:** Tremendous shorebreak during heavy surf.

Cameo Shores Cove
Infrequent peaks that break over a ragged rocky shelf. Ridable on any swell from 2-5 feet. Medium tide. **Note:** Area is private and public access is prohibited . . . rarely worth the hassle anyway.

Scotchman's Cove
Privately owned, but public admitted for a fee. Surf is small and inconsistent. Only ridable during big south swells. Nothing in winter. **Comment:** Good swimming and bodysurfing during summer months.

Rockpile
Inconsistent reef peaks in front of the Laguna Art Gallery. Surfable all year from 3-6 feet. Medium tide. Heavy surf usually closes out.

SOUTHERN CALIFORNIA

Laguna Beach
A series of small offshore reefs producing two-way peaks. Breaks along a ½ mile of sand and rock beachfront. Takes any swell but is best on a 3-6 foot west. Medium tide. Strong south swells close out. Heavy crowds during summer.
Note: The popular streets are St. Anns, Thalia, Anita, and Oak. **Comment:** Fantastic bodysurfing after the boards leave.

Brooks Street
Thick peaks build over submerged reefs and peel left for about 200 yards. Breaks best on 3-10 foot south swell. Favors a medium tide. Winter is typical beach surf. **Caution:** Rocks in breakline and on the beach . . . watch the tide. Also, strong upcoast currents during heavy summer surf. **Note:** Fabulous bodysurfing after boards leave. **Comment:** The cleanest, best-shaped big wave in Laguna Beach.

Victoria Cove/Aliso Creek/Camel Point
Public beaches . . . clean and sandy. Good bodysurfing. Ridable during a big south swell. Best at medium-high tide. **Comment:** Strong shorebreak in shallow water - for expert swimmers only.

BROOKS STREET . . at its best during a south swell.

A small reef wave in LAGUNA BEACH.

DANA STRAND on an unusually well-shaped day. Note: It rarely gets this good.

"The Point" of SALT CREEK. They can ruin the beach, but they can't stop the surf.

Unreal shorebreak at SALT CREEK.

SALT CREEK

For years this beach was a raw, undeveloped park with easy access. The area is now under development and direct public access is threatened. There are 2 major surfing areas:

The Point: Lines peak in front of the south point and peel smoothly left. Breaks best during a strong south swell with medium tide. Ridable from 3-15 feet. A paddling channel runs just north of the breakline. **Caution:** Strong up-coast currents and shorebreak during heavy surf.

The Beach: A long stretch of beach surf north of "The Point". Shape is unpredictable — depends on contour of the sand bottom. Takes any swell. Medium tide. Ridable from 2-5 feet. Larger surf usually closes out.
Note: Niguel Beach Park provides beach access (see map). Salt Creek is a mile north.

Dana Strand

Deep water peaks that end in a crushing shorebreak. Breaks on any swell. Medium-low tide. Private beach front. **Note:** Public stairs at Niguel Beach Park provide access. **Comment:** A marshmellow shoulder . . . rarely worth the walk.

Perfect trim at "the point" of SALT CREEK.

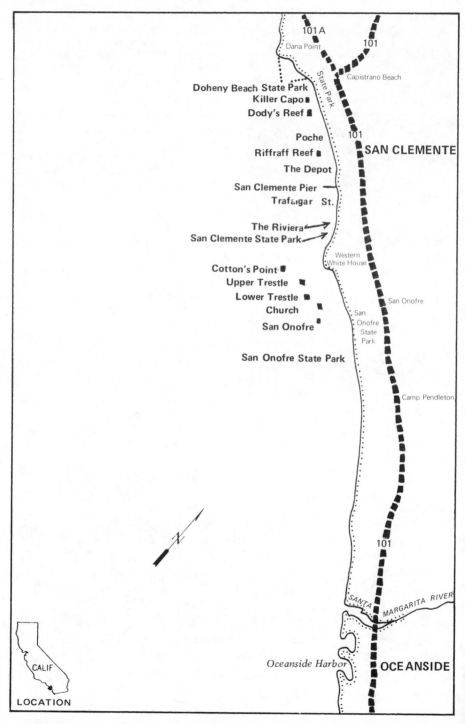

101 A
Dana Point
101
State Park
Capistrano Beach

Doheny Beach State Park
Killer Capo
Dody's Reef

Poche
Riffraff Reef
The Depot
San Clemente Pier
Trafalgar St.

101
SAN CLEMENTE

The Riviera
San Clemente State Park

Western
White House

Cotton's Point
Upper Trestle
Lower Trestle
Church
San Onofre

San
Onofre
State
Park

San Onofre

San Onofre State Park

Camp Pendleton

101

SANTA MARGARITA RIVER

CALIF

LOCATION

Oceanside Harbor

OCEANSIDE

A clean west line peels into the SAN CLEMENTE PIER.

There aren't many left but this is one of them — "A secret spot".

Doheny Beach State Park

The mellow lines of Doheny are all but gone. Replaced by the calm water of Dana Point Harbor. But still . . . small peaks and lines during a south swell. Gentle and easy-breaking. Excellent for beginners. Works from 1-5 feet, medium-low tide. Sandy beach. Rock bottom! Very few hazards. **Note:** Camping is allowed in state park. But make reservations in advance.

Killer Capo

A thick, lonesome peak breaking ¼ mile off Capistrano beach. Vertical drops that suddenly shoulder to nothing. Takes a west swell. Ridable from 6-18 feet. Low tide. **Note:** Private beachfront - enter from Doheny and walk south. **Comment:** A favorite for the local Hobie Cats.

Dody's Reef

Big, outside peaks. Takes a strong south or west swell. Breaks ½ mile south of Killer Capo. **Comment:** Very unpredictable . . . rarely ridden.

Poche

Smooth peelers - right or left. Easy peaks and lines across an outside reef. Breaks on any swell. Makeable from 2-10 feet. Shape better at low tide. **Note:** Private beach - Access is restricted to members and guests of beach club. Enter from public beaches to the north or south.

Riffraff Reef

Temperamental peaks and lines. Breaks in front of a private trailer park. Takes any swell. Any tide. **Comment:** Direct access restricted. Usually not worth the trouble anyway.

SOUTHERN CALIFORNIA

The Depot
Pop-up beach peaks in front of an old train station. Ridable on any swell from 1-4 feet. Strong lines close out. Sandy beach and bottom. **Comment:** Early mornings at a medium tide are your best bet.

San Clemente Pier
Peak surf on both sides of pier. North side is favored. Breaks best on a 2-8 foot peaky winter swell. Strong summer swells close out. Best at medium tide. **Comment:** Also has excellent bodysurfing, paipo boarding, knee boarding, etc. . . . A popular summertime beach.

Trafalgar Street
An outside reef break - ¼ mile south of pier. Thick peaks with smooth lefts and rights. Lefts are usually better shaped. Takes any swell and is ridable from 2-8 feet. Becomes a bit tubular as tide drops. Sandy beach and bottom. **Note:** Great bodysurfing . . . once the boards have left.

The Trestle Lady.

This is all that's left of the famous surf of DOHENY BEACH. The perfect peelers are gone forever.

TRAFALGAR STREET is one of the main surfing areas in San Clemente. It breaks all year but is best in summer. Peaks like this are common during south swells.

Winter peaks at UPPER TRESTLE — seen from Hwy 101.

The Riviera

Typical California beach surf, ¼ mile north of the state park. Works on any swell - summer or winter. Ridable from 1-4 feet after that . . . forget it. Occasionally fast and hollow. Medium-low tide usually best.

San Clemente State Park

Small, little peaks in front of park's main beach. Breaks on most swells from 2-5 feet. Anything bigger and it closes out. Shape usually best at a medium tide. **Note:** Great camping facilities are available in state park.

Cotton's Point

The old Cotton Estate is no longer . . . times have changed. But the big lefts still rumble off San Mateo Point. Strong south swells focus onto a reef nearly ½ mile from shore. Thick walls suddenly suck up into vertical peaks then peel smoothly left until they explode in a crushing shorebreak. Needs at least 6 feet to break and is ridable to 15 or more. Any tide is OK but medium is preferred. A paddling channel runs north of breakline. Rock bottom sandy beach. **Caution:** Strong rip currents and frequent cleanup sets . . . take heed! **Note:** Access is restricted and heavily guarded. **Comment:** A powerful wave - very dangerous during large surf. Experienced riders only.

SAN ONOFRE . . . 1965. This once private stretch of shoreline is now open to the public.

A glassy west swell unwinds off the point at UPPER TRESTLE.

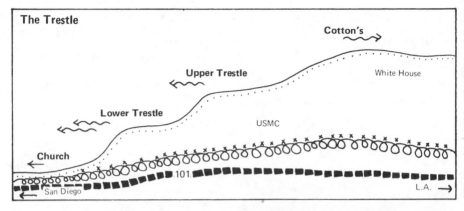

LOWER TRESTLE. Although best known for its summer surf, it has winter surf too. This photo was taken in February during a 6-8 foot **west** swell.

Upper Trestle

Mainly a winter break - has summer surf too. Long, well-shaped rights off a rocky point. 150 yds. south of Cotton's. Breaks on any swell but a clean west produces the best shape. South swells tend to section and close out. Takeoffs are steep and hairy followed by a thick, hardbreaking wall. Ridable from 2-12 feet. Medium-low tide. Rock bottom with a sandy beach. **Comment:** Winter's replacement for Lower Trestle.

Lower Trestle

A classic summer break. Perfect right lines peeling off a point. Takeoffs are very steep followed by long, tube-like wall. Numerous hollow sections appear as wave nears shore. Ridable from 2 feet and up but doesn't cook until it nears 6 plus. A medium-low tide supplies some juice. Rock bottom. Sandy beach. **Note:** For years the Marine Corps has made this area off limits to the public. Now, after years of hassle, a portion will be opened for public use.
Comment: The floodgates are open . . . the Trestle will soon look like Malibu - a wall to wall body jam.

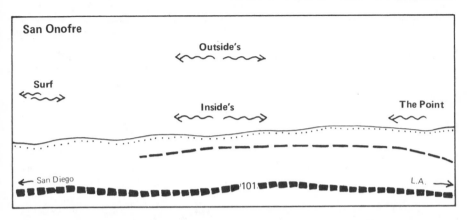

San Onofre

Outside's

Surf

Inside's

The Point

← San Diego   '101.   L.A. →

Top: CHURCH. Bottom: San Onofre Creek.

The peaks of SAN ONOFRE STATE PARK.

Church

Long, well-shaped right lines. Breaks over a submerged rock point ½ mile south of Lower Trestle. Small surf is slow and easy. Strong lines pack the punch. Shape is best during winter on any north or west swell. Medium tide. Rock bottom, sandy beach. **Comment:** A good spot if the Trestle is too crowded.

SAN ONOFRE

Two miles of rugged, undeveloped coastline. For years this area was used only by the San Onofre Surfing Club. But now its open to the public. The following reefs produce year'round surf:

The Point

Fast, zippy rights and lefts. Breaks over a small rock point, ¼ mile north of main beach. Takes any swell but the shape is best during winter months. Ridable from 2-6 feet. Medium-low tide. Rock bottom - sandy beach. **Comment:** The only "juice" break at San Onofre.

Inside's

Small, shifty peaks. Breaks from 1-4 feet - year'round. Any tide is OK. Few hazards. **Comment:** A safe place for the kids to learn.

Outside's

Thick, two-way peaks — 300-400 yards offshore. Vertical drops onto wide mushy shoulders. Breaks on any swell but favors a strong south. Ridable from 4 feet on up. Medium-low tide. **Comment:** Looks easy . . . but waves are big and the swims are long. No place for beginners.

San Onofre State Park

A newly opened state park. Miles of white sandy beach and unridden reef breaks. Peaks set up and break in consistent patterns. Rights and lefts that peel cleanly into deep channels. Ridable at any size any tide. Breaks summer or winter. **Note:** Overnight camping allowed. **Comment:** Uncrowded, unsurfed tubes and shoulders.

143

SOUTHERN CALIFORNIA

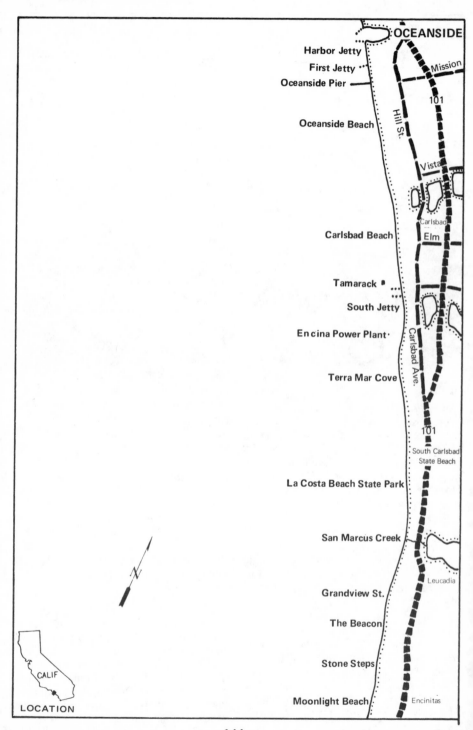

OCEANSIDE

Harbor Jetty

First Jetty

Oceanside Pier

Mission

101

Hill St.

Oceanside Beach

Vista

Carlsbad

Carlsbad Beach

Elm

Tamarack

South Jetty

Encina Power Plant

Carlsbad Ave.

Terra Mar Cove

101

South Carlsbad
State Beach

La Costa Beach State Park

San Marcus Creek

Leucadia

Grandview St.

The Beacon

Stone Steps

Moonlight Beach

Encinitas

N

CALIF

LOCATION

Harbor Jetty
Right lines breaking across sandbars just below south seawall. Works best on a north or west swell. Ridable from 2-6 feet. Medium tide usually best. Bottom and beach are both sandy. **Comment:** A safe place when the surf is small.

First Jetty
Fast little tubes breaking on both sides of a rock jetty. A winter break. Best on a 2-5 foot west swell. Medium-low tide. Bigger surf closes out. **Comment:** Ideal when the warm offshores blow out of the dry desert canyons.

FIRST JETTY . . . south side.

FIRST JETTY . . . north side.

Oceanside Beach. A low tide tube at "First Jetty".

OCEANSIDE PIER. Waves like this break both at the pier and along the beach.

A cold winter line unwinds at CARLSBAD BEACH.

Although best in summer, TAMARACK also breaks during winter. This photo was taken in January during a small, well-shaped west swell.

Oceanside Pier
Peaks and lines on either side of pier. Shape depends on contour of shifting sand bottom. Works on any swell from 2-8 feet. Fast and tubular at low tide. Soft and mushy at high tide. **Comment:** Always something breaking - summer or winter.

Oceanside Beach
3 miles of wide open beach surf. Pop-up peaks with two-way lines. Breaks year'-round - always has surf. Ridable from 1-8 feet . . . then it closes out. Medium-low tide usually best. Sand bottom and beach. **Comment:** Consistent surf - both summer and winter.

Carlsbad Beach
Normal beach waves. Similar to those found in Oceanside. Ridable all year. Never too crowded. Shape varys according to contour of sand bottom. **Comment:** A dependable year'round beach break.

Tamarack
Offshore reefs produce super clean peaks. Easy takeoffs with mellow right and left lines. Best in summer on a 2-8 foot south swell. Breaks winter too but shape not as good. Medium tide is best. **Comment:** A popular spot - if there's a swell Tamarack will have the shape.

South Jetty

Soft rights that peel cleanly from a central peak. An easy takeoff followed by a thick, fading shoulder. Ridable from 2-5 feet. Any winter swell. Breaks summer too. **Note:** Located just south of small jetties at entrance to Agua Hedionda Lagoon.

Encina Power Plant

Long summer lefts just north of the private village of Terra Mar. Needs a healthy 6-12 foot south swell and low tide. **Comment:** Pumps and grinds when its big. Small surf is powerless.

The jetty south of TAMARACK.

Terra Mar Cove

A rarely surfed reef break directly in front of Terra Mar. Ridable from 3-10 feet during winter swells. Needs low tide. **Note:** No direct access - enter from public beaches to the north or south.

La Costa Beach State Park

Mild peaks with slow shouldering lines. Breaks all year but boogies during a heavy south. Ridable from 2-10 feet. Medium low tide. Heavy crowds during summertime. **Note:** Overnight camping in park if you can get in. Usually a 2 month wait during summer.

LA COSTA PARK.

San Marcus Creek

Fast, hot tubes up and down the beach. Needs a 1-4 foot peaky west swell. Medium-low tide. Larger surf usually closes out. Located south of La Costa Park - look for creek marker along highway. **Comment:** Shape is usually best after a heavy rain when sandbars have had a chance to form.

Winter waves at MOONLIGHT BEACH.

Leucadia

Two miles of soft, easy breaking beach surf. Ridable on any swell from 2-6 feet. Medium-low tide. Larger swells (6+) line up and close out. Sand bottom and beach. The popular breaks include: **Grandview Street, The Beacon,** and **Stone Steps.** See map for locations.

Moonlight Beach

Typical beach surf. Thick peaks with wide, easy shoulders. Lots of room for jammin. Works on any swell but shape favors a south. Ridable up to 6 feet. Medium tide is best.

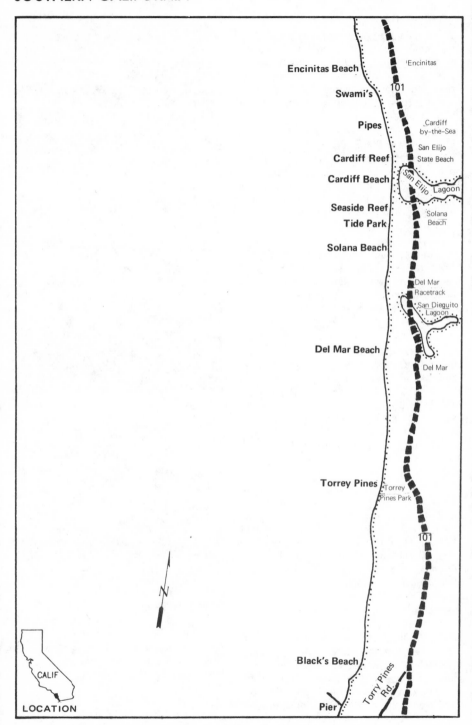

Encinitas Beach

Encinitas

101

Swami's

Pipes

Cardiff by-the-Sea

San Elijo State Beach

Cardiff Reef

Cardiff Beach

San Elijo Lagoon

Seaside Reef

Solana Beach

Tide Park

Solana Beach

Del Mar Racetrack

San Dieguito Lagoon

Del Mar Beach

Del Mar

Torrey Pines

Torrey Pines Park

101

Black's Beach

Torrey Pines Rd.

Pier

N

CALIF

LOCATION

SWAMI's . . . small and very crowded.

"The Boneyard" at SWAMI's.

An 8 foot west swell rolls off the point at SWAMI'S. Normal lineup is to far right of photo. These surfers are way out of position.

Encinitas Beach
A mile or more of uncrowded beach surf. Soft breaking peaks with smooth two-way lineups. Breaks on any swell but favors a south. A medium tide is preferred. **Note:** Steep cliffs prevent direct access. Enter from Moonlight or Swami's.

Swami's
A classic winter break. Vertical takeoffs with thick right lines . . . long and mellow. Peels smoothly for nearly ¼ mile. Needs a 4-12 foot north or west swell. Medium-low tide. Small surf is well-shaped but very sectiony.

The outer point is referred to as **THE BONEYARD.** Takes the same swell and tide but is never as crowded as main point. **Comment:** A primo winter break.

When heavy winter surf hits, SWAMI'S is the place to ride. It can handle any size swell.

149

SOUTHERN CALIFORNIA

Pipes
Hollow beach peaks . . . ½ miles south of Swami's. Usually steep and tubular. Breaks on any swell but favors a west. Ridable from 2-10 feet. **Note:** Camping allowed in San Elijo Park. **Comment:** Fast and hollow no matter what the tide.

Cardiff Reef
Mild peaks with shouldering rights and lefts. Breaks ¼ mile offshore. Well--formed but usually slow and mushy. Breaks all year - any swell. Super on a west. Tide makes little difference. Ridable up to 8 feet, after that it closes out. Paddling channels on both sides of the reef. Breaks in front of the San Elijo Creek trestle.

Cardiff Beach
A mile of pop-up beach peaks. Located between Cardiff Reef and Seaside Reef. Mellow takeoffs with tapering right and left lines. Breaks all year - any swell. Ridable from 2-6 feet. A strong west swell produces best shape. Favors a medium-low tide. **Comment:** Peaks everywhere - just pick the one that's working best.

Top: PIPES. Bottom: SAN ELIJO PARK.

CARDIFF REEF breaking both ways.

CARDIFF BEACH. This is what can result from a west swell at medium-low tide.

150

SEASIDE REEF . . . smooth and easy.

TORREY PINES STATE PARK.

Morning lines at DEL MAR BEACH.

Seaside Reef
A steep, centered peak that explodes over a shallow rock reef. Peels left or right for a short ways then gradually backs off as it enters deep water. Plenty of room to manuever. Best on a 3-6 foot south swell. Any tide O.K. **Note:** Shoreline area is private - enter from public beach north of break.

Tide Park
Heavy peaks breaking over a flatrock ledge - ¼ mile off the beach. Slow right lines (some lefts). Never really pumps. Needs a 6 foot swell to break and is still ridable at 15. Huge south swells give it juice. Stays glassy most of the day.**Caution:** Jagged rocks and large, mansize holes lurk below the surface. Extremely dangerous at low tide.

Solana Beach
Sheer cliffs hinder access to the uncrowded waves of Solana. Lines peak on outside reefs forming mild, easy-breaking rights and lefts. Takes any swell - summer or winter. Ridable from 2-6 feet. Best at medium tide. **Note:** A peaky west swell makes the place cook.

Del Mar Beach
Another 3 miles of typical beach surf. Similar to that of Solana. Smooth peaks and two-way shoulders. Breaks all year but is best on a strong south. Ridable from 2-8 feet. Medium tide. **Comment:** Well-shaped surf can usually be found at the end of any seaward side street.

Torrey Pines
4½ miles of high-powered peaks. Unnamed and rarely ridden. Takes any swell from 2-15 feet. Favors a strong south and medium tide. Holds shape in large surf - the problem then is getting out. **Caution:** Many hazards - use extreme caution and never surf alone.

The low tide juice — SOLANA BEACH.

SOUTHERN CALIFORNIA

This photograph explains why the surf at BLACK'S BEACH breaks so hard. In the center, where no waves are breaking, is the Scripp's Branch of the famous La Jolla Submarine Canyon. This ravine is almost a mile deep and runs slightly off the La Jolla shoreline. Because of this depth, fast moving ocean swells meet no resistance as they sweep shoreward. The first object they contact is a shallow reef (seen near top of photo). It's no wonder that with such unrestrained speed and power the surf breaks so hard and fast.

BLACK'S BEACH . . . A gnarly 12 feet.

Black's Beach

At onetime a "secret" spot . . . now heavily surfed. Thick, explosive peaks that break all year. Steep, top-to-bottom takeoffs with hollow, spitting lefts and rights. Ridable on any swell from 2-15 feet. Backwash at high tide — medium-low preferred. Steep cliffs and private property restrict access . . . but there are ways in. **Note:** Shape is best during strong south swells. **Caution:** Strong rip currents during heavy surf . . . no place for beginners. **Comment:** One of the most powerful beach breaks in all of California. Respect its power.

A BLACK's peak . . . top-to-bottom.

152

Riding the tight backside line at BLACK'S BEACH . . . Rider has successfully negotiated the vertical drop and is about to accelerate up and into the pocket. Note the massive explosion taking place to his right. Its big and gnarly. A typical day at Black's.

BLACK'S BEACH — Peaks like this break all along Black's Beach. No matter what the swell or what the tide there is always surf. In this photo, two knee boarders were almost caught inside. The one on the left has already scrambled up the face and broken through the lip (note foam trail to left of center). The one on the right is still frantically kicking as the lip begins to hook. Note the wave's extreme concave shape and the thickness of the lip. Also note the perfect shoulders, right or left.

SOUTHERN CALIFORNIA

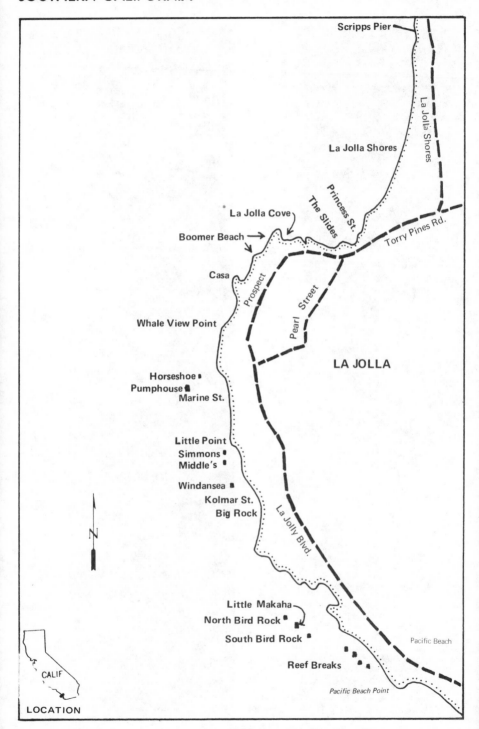

Scripps Pier

La Jolla Shores

La Jolla Shores

Torry Pines Rd.

Princess St.

The Slides

La Jolla Cove

Boomer Beach →

Casa

Prospect

Pearl Street

Whale View Point

LA JOLLA

Horseshoe ▪
Pumphouse ▪
Marine St.

Little Point ▪
Simmons ▪
Middle's ▪

Windansea ▪
Kolmar St.
Big Rock

La Jolly Blvd.

N

Little Makaha
North Bird Rock ▪
South Bird Rock ▪

Pacific Beach

Reef Breaks

Pacific Beach Point

CALIF

LOCATION

SCRIPPS PIER — north side.

Looking south from SCRIPPS.

Scripps Pier

Thick, sandbar peaks on both sides of pier. North side is favored. Best on a west swell at medium-low tide. Ridable from 2-6 feet. Large surf closes out. Sandy beach and bottom.

La Jolla Shores

Typical beach surf. Well-shaped during the winter months. Ridable from 2-6 feet. Lines up when it gets big. Medium tide preferred. Usually glassy till late mornings. **Comment:** Very reliable . . . always has some kind of surf.

Princess Street

Small reef waves breaking off a private beach. Works on any winter swell from 2-5 feet. Medium tide is safest. Rocks everywhere. **Comment:** Very temperamental - rarely worth the ½ mile walk from the Shores.

The Slides

Rights and lefts below sheer cliffs. Slow, bumpy and very sectiony. Rocks everywhere. Works best on 3-8 foot winter swell. Medium tide. **Comment:** Requires a long walk from the Shores. Usually not worth the hassle.

A "close out" set — LA JOLLA SHORES.

The small beach surf of LA JOLLA.

BIG ROCK . . . Note deflection angle of soup. It's shallow.

BIG ROCK . . . two knee boarders move into lineup.

SOUTHERN CALIFORNIA

La Jolla Cove

The "big-wave" break of La Jolla. Needs a strong 8-20 foot winter swell before it cooks. Thick, vertical peaks with long left walls. Rocks and cliffs await lost boards and bodies. Any tide OK but a medium-low is safest. **Note:** Watch for huge section which appears soon after takeoff. **Comment:** Doesn't happen often but when it does . . . it pumps.

Boomer Beach

North: A bodysurfing break . . . no surfing allowed. A vertical peak with a thick right shoulder. Ends in a violent shorebreak. Needs a strong winter swell. Rocks . . . medium tide is safe. **Note:** For experts only.

South: Thick left shoulders from a central peak. Needs a winter swell and medium tide. Erratic shape — rarely ridable. **Note:** Bodysurfing only . . . no boards allowed.

Casa

A gnarly winter wall - ¼ mile from shore. Breaks from top to bottom over a razor sharp reef. Needs a 6-15 foot winter swell. High tide. **Note:** Rarely (if ever) surfed.

Whale View Point

Gnarly summer lefts off a rocky point. Needs a straight 3-10 foot south swell and high tide. Bumpy and inconsistent during winter months. **Caution:** Dangerous rocks . . . watch the tide.

Horseshoe

Strong south swells produce thick, left walls that pump and grind across a shallow reef. Takes a 6-12 foot swell to break. Favors medium tide. Just north of Marine Street. **Comment:** Real summer juice.

Pumphouse

Large winter swells produce thick left and right walls. Breaks on a deep reef - ¼ mile outside Marine Street. Needs 6 feet or more. Medium tide. **Caution:** Strong currents during heavy surf. Use extreme caution.

SOUTH BOOMER.

NORTH BOOMER.

A thick line at the LA JOLLA COVE . . . 1963. The slightly feathering lip (extreme right) indicates a watery section thats about to descend.

A short paddle above Windansea is a big-wave break called MIDDLES.

The takeoffs at SIMMON'S are steep . . . as this surfer will attest to. Note also what awaits lost boards.

Marine Street
Bodysurfing shorebreak. Breaks 'all year but smooth and warm in summer. Sandy bottom. A popular summer beach. **Caution:** During times of heavy surf, strong rip-currents develop near shore.

Little Point
A fast summer left. Breaks off a small rock point just north of Simmons. Takes a 2-8 foot south swell. Rocky shoreline - medium-high tide advisable. **Comment:** "A smoking little tube".

Simmons
A sucking peak takeoff folowed by a tubular right line. Explodes in only 2 feet of water then quickly peels along a rock ledge. Needs at least a 5 foot west swell and medium-high tide.

Middle's
Wintertime's answer to Windansea. Thick lines that peak on an outside reef and push slowly shoreward. Wave backs off in deep water before reaching the beach. Needs an 8-15 foot swell before it breaks. Any tide is O.K. **Comment:** Thick and mushy - well suited for long boards and old-timers.

1963 . . . Three friends enjoying "the good ol days" at the "main peak" of WINDANSEA. Ones going right, ones going left, and the one in the middle is going to eat it . . . Those days are gone — only memories. But the main peak isn't! It's still there, producing surf as good as ever.

Windansea

Summer: A class summer break. Steep shifting peaks with strong left shoulders. Occasional rights. Takes a south or west swell. Best from 4 feet and up. Ridable at any tide. **Caution:** Strong currents and shorebreak during heavy surf! **Note:** Usually 2-3 feet bigger than rest of coast. **Comment:** A primo summer spot . . . usually very crowded.

Winter: Northern lines peak on the outside reefs and gradually move to shore . . . . breaking - rebuilding - then breaking again. Works on any winter swell from 2-12 feet. Any tide. **Comment:** A roomy, workable wave.

Kolmar Street

Fast, little reef waves - 20 yds. off a sandy beach. Breaks on any swell from 2-6 feet. Heavy lines close out. Medium tide best. **Note:** Regulated surfing check with lifeguards.

Big Rock

A spitting tube. Peaks on a shallow reef then grinds left along a rock ledge. Works on any swell from 2-10 feet. **Caution:** Reef is razor sharp. A medium-high tide is a must. **Comment:** The initial drop is a bit touchy, but once turned it's time to boogie.

Nothing has changed at BIG ROCK. Compare this photo with the two at the bottom of page 155. Note the similarity of shape and speed even though this one is much larger.

Water level at NORTH BIRD ROCK around 1961. Two surfers drive into the main peak while rider in foreground fades left as he lines up the big but mushy right.

Little Makaha

Watery lines breaking nearly ½ mile from shore. Thick peaks with mushy, slow-breaking shoulders. Works both summer and winter. Needs a 6-20 foot swell and a medium-low tide. **Comment:** Big waves only. Breaks only 2 or 3 times a year.

North Bird Rock

A thick concentrated peak - ½ mile from shore. Breaks top-to-bottom with a strong right or left wall to follow. Needs an 8-20 foot south or southwest swell. Low tide. Beach and bottom both rocky but surf backs off before reaching shore. **Note:** Only breaks 2 or 3 times a year. **Comment:** The class big-wave of La Jolla when it works.

South Bird Rock

Clean summer surf. Mild peaks with easy right and left set ups. Fast sections at low tide. Breaks hard during large swells. Thick kelp keeps it glassy. Ridable from 3-10 feet on any swell. South swells are best.

Reef Breaks

Numerous small reef breaks found between South Bird and Pacific Beach Point. They break year'round - summer or winter. Usually ridable from 2-6 feet. Bigger swells close out. Sharp rocks everywhere - wait for high tide. **Note:** Area is private . . . no direct access . . . a real hassle.

An old photo of the easy peaks at SOUTH BIRD. La Jolla, California.

SOUTHERN CALIFORNIA

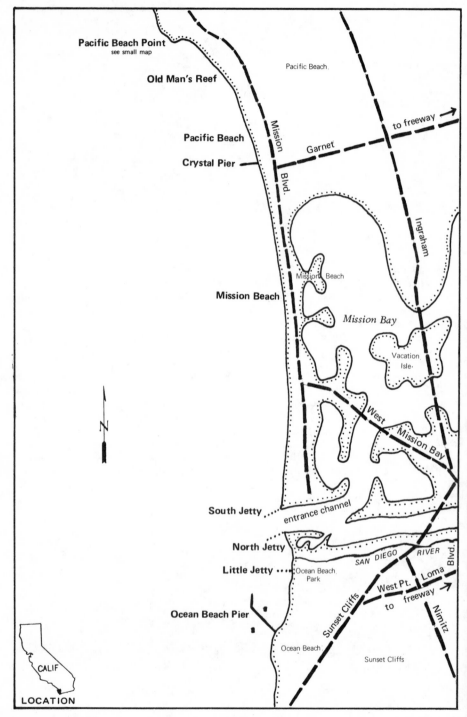

Pacific Beach Point
see small map

Old Man's Reef

Pacific Beach.

to freeway

Pacific Beach

Crystal Pier

Mission Blvd.

Garnet

Ingraham

Mission Beach

Mission Beach

Mission Bay

Vacation Isle.

N

West Mission Bay

South Jetty

entrance channel

North Jetty

SAN DIEGO RIVER

Little Jetty

Ocean Beach Park

West Pt.

Loma Blvd.

Sunset Cliffs

to freeway

Nimitz

Ocean Beach Pier

Ocean Beach.

Sunset Cliffs

CALIF

LOCATION

PACIFIC BEACH POINT

A series of reef breaks extending from Pacific Point to Tourmaline Surfing Park. Ridable all year but best during winter months. Breaks on any swell from 2-6 feet. Medium tide. Rocks and steep cliffs along beach . . . not dangerous. The surfable peaks are:

Outside's

A right off the outer point. Short but usually well-shaped. Best on a 2-8 foot west swell. Medium-low tide. Sections as it nears main point.

The Point

Easy rights and lefts off the main point. Breaks with very little power. Best on 2-6 foot west swel. Medium-low tide.

Inside's

Two-way peaks. Soft takeoffs with easy breaking lines. Unmakable sections at low tide. Plenty of room . . . never very crowded.

Old Man's Reef

Soft two-way peaks. Breaks year'round. Best on a west swell. Ridable from 2-8 feet. Medium tide. **Comment:** A favorite of oldtimers and longboarders.

Pacific Beach

Two miles of beach peaks. Shape changes daily. Breaks on any swell from 2-6 feet. Medium tide. Closes out when surf gets big. **Note:** Surfing regulations during summer months . . . see lifeguards.

Crystal Pier

Normal sandbar peaks. Occasionally better shape than rest of beach. Breaks year'round on any swell. Ridable from 2-6 feet. Medium tide. **Comment:** A favorite spot for locals of Pacific and Mission Beach.

West swells at PACIFIC BEACH POINT.

The "south" jetty of MISSION BEACH.

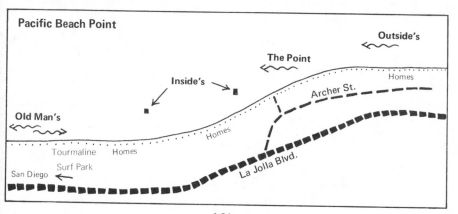

A winter line sparkles off the CRYSTAL PIER.

The surf of MISSION BEACH. In background is the crowded shoreline of Pacific Beach. Note: photo was taken from the "south jetty".

Mission Beach
Another mile or so of uncrowded beach surf. Works on any swell. Usually has best shape at medium tide. Ridable from 2-5 feet. Fabulous swimming and bodysurfing during summer months. Sandy beach and bottom. **Caution:** Watch out for strong upcoast currents during heavy surf.

South Jetty
Two-way peaks breaking off the north seawall. Mainly lefts - some rights. Shifting peaks here and there. Best in winter during a 2-8 foot north/west swell. Medium tide. Sand bottom and beach. **Note:** The last spot in San Diego area to blow out. Usually ridable till late morning.

"Cowabunga" . . .

162

Although it's called NORTH JETTY this is actually the south jetty of the entrance channel to Mission Bay. For more information see the map on page 160 and the description below.

The "Little Jetty" of OCEAN BEACH.

The OCEAN BEACH PIER — north side.

North Jetty
Shifty sandbar peaks with fast (sometimes hollow) rights. Breaks off the **south** seawall of the entrance to Mission Bay. Takes any swell but is superior on a 2-8 foot west. Medium-low tide. **Comment:** A dependable spot - always has surf of some kind.

Little Jetty
Small, shifty beach peaks. Makeable from 1-5 feet then closes out. Takes any swell. Medium tide best. Sandy bottom. **Note:** Always has some kind of surf - a good beginner's break.

Ocean Beach Pier
Powerful right peaks - **north** side of pier. Needs a 2-10 foot west swell. Medium-low tide. Paddling channel next to pier . . . Also:
An outer reef just **south** of pier. Easy, slow moving lefts toward pilings. Takes any swell from 2-6 feet. Medium tide. **Caution:** Rocks and cliffs start just south of pier.

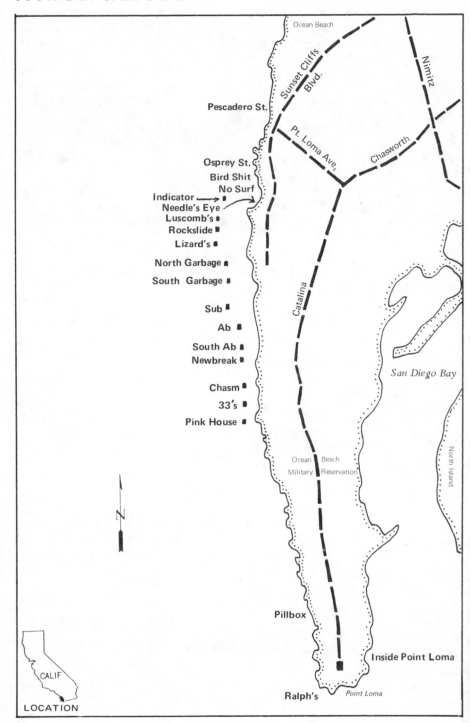

Pescadero Street

A good beginners spot. Slow, easy rights and lefts. Breaks on both sides of a deep channel. Best during winter on a 2-6 foot west swell. Medium tide. Sandy beach at low tide. Few hazards.

Osprey Street

Deceptive peaks that look soft but break with force. Peaks over an inside reef and peels right toward a jutting rock point. Breaks on most swells but best on a 2-8 foot west. Medium-low tide. **Caution:** Sheer cliffs and rocks - no beach.

Bird Shit

Small lefts breaking off an inside reef. Works on any winter swell from 2-5 feet. Bumpy at higher tides - needs medium-low. Cliffs and rocks along shoreline. Enter at Osprey and paddle south.

No Surf

Junk surf off an inside reef. Located between Bird Shit and Needles Eye. Small, inconsistent peaks. Rarely worth getting wet for.

Indicator

The outer reef of Bird Shit. Long, peeling lefts. Needs at least a 5 foot swell - west preferred. Best at medium-low tide.

Lines peel into OSPREY STREET

The lineup at NORTH GARBAGE.

PILL BOX reef — Pt. Loma.

A flat day at RALPHS.

ROCKSLIDE lefts . . . bumpy but still ridable.

ROCKSIDE breaks both ways. Today, the lefts are cook'n.

Needles Eye
Fast lefts over an inside reef. Takes a south or southwest swell. Ridable from 2-5 feet - anything bigger closes out. **Note:** Gets name from rock pinnacles near shore.

Luscomb's
Solid rights and lefts off an outer reef - ¼ mile offshore. Thick peaks with fast lineups - depending on the tide. Best during a 3-10 foot west swell. Low tide gives it juice.

Rockslide
Strong peaks - right and left. Meaty takeoffs with thick, fast lines. Breaks on any swell but a 2-8 foot west is the best. Medium-low tide. Return channels on both sides of breakline. Breaks on the outer reef — 100 yds. below Luscombs.

Lizard's
Lefts off a small reef sandwiched between Rockslide and North Garbage. Usually very bumpy. Occasionally well-shaped. **Comment:** Tempermental - a "sometimes" break.

SOUTH GARBAGE is but a short paddle south of North Garbage. If one isn't working the other usually is.

LUSCOMB'S . . . two coming in — three heading out.

North Garbage
Strong two-way lines from a central peak. Mild lineups that quickly encounter fast inside sections. Breaks best during winter months. Medium-low tide. Ridable from 2-10 feet. **Note:** Located in front of Ladera Street.

South Garbage
Breaks like North Garbage only the lineups are a bit longer. Take any winter swell. Ridable from 3-10 feet. Medium-low tide. **Note:** Named for the large amount of "garbage" that floats in the side channels.

Sub
Thick, two-way lines. Bumpy and unreliable. Breaks on any swell - summer or winter. Ridable from 3-10 feet. Best when the winds have died and the tide is out. **Comment:** Very tempermental -

Ab
Long, meaty lefts - some rights. Thick takeoffs followed by a well-shaped but slow lineup. Needs a south or west swell. Ridable from 2-8 feet. Medium-low tide. Access is either by foot or a steep rope drop off cliff. **Note:** Can be checked from Cal Western parking lot.

The afternoon chop has begun to settle as this rider screams across a LUSCOMBS Left.

A clean west swell peels across AB'S reef. It's nearing dark and there s only I surfer still out (his head is visible at right center of photo). Picture was taken from the parking lot at Cal. Western — a college in Pt. Loma.

AB. Surfer from the above photo is calling it quits. The lefts are still makeable but are beginning to line across to SUB (the next reef north).

South Ab

Thick lines that peak and peel both right and left. The right is usually better. Takes any winter swell. Medium-low tide. Breaks from 2-10 feet then closes out. **Note:** It is sometimes makeable from South Ab, through New Break's peak and into the normal New Break lineup . . . but very rare.

New Break

Primo rights that peel off a submerged rock point. Thick peak takeoffs followed by a well-shaped lineup that passes through 2 or 3 sections. Takes any winter swell - prefers a west. Best from 3-10 feet. Wave speed depends on tide . . . Medium-low the best.

NEW BREAK. Considered by many as the best wave south of Ladera Street. It is seen here during a 4-6 foot west swell at medium-low tide.

Foreground: A NEW BREAK right nears its end. Background: A CHASM left nears its end. In the center: A paddling channel for either break.

Chasm

Smooth lefts. Breaks across the channel from New Break. Lines peak on an outer reef and peel cleanly along a rock ledge. Larger waves sometimes connect with New Break. Works best on a 2-8 foot west swell. Medium-low tide.

33's

Isolated peaks. More than a mile south of Ladera Street. Breaks year'round. Best during winter. Medium tide. **Comment:** A long walk but usually worth it. it.

Pink House

Thick, two-way peaks that peel across a jagged rock shelf. Breaks on any swell from 2-10 feet. **Note:** Accessible by boat only.

Pill Box

A small, concentrated peak with a flat right and left shoulder. Never crowded - access is by boat only. Takes away any swell from 2-10 feet. Medium-low tide. **Caution:** Shark country . . . keep alert. **Note:** Can be checked from the Cabrillo National Monument . . . on the cliffs above.

Ralphs

Long "Malibu-type" rights off the tip of Point Loma. South swells generate flawless tubes. Ridable from 2-10 feet. Medium-low tide. No direct access - can only be reached by boat. **Caution:** Sharks feed at mouth of harbor - use extreme caution. **Comment:** One of the last uncrowded point breaks in California.

SOUTHERN CALIFORNIA

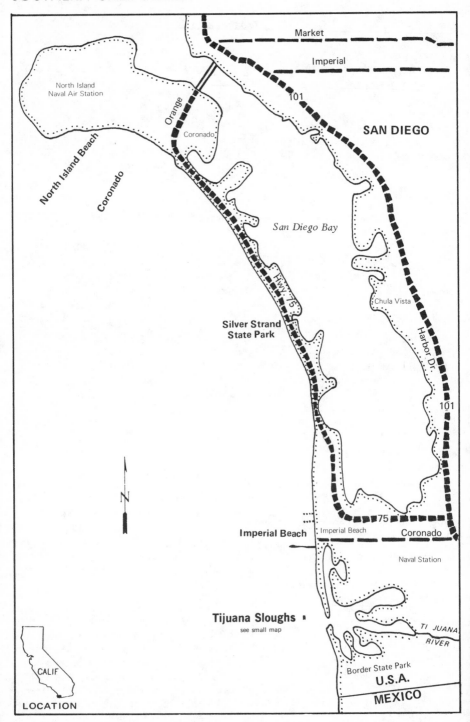

IMPERIAL BEACH PIER — north side.

IMPERIAL BEACH PIER — south side.

North Island Beach

A military reservation - access restricted. A mile or more of rarely ridden beach waves. Breaks on any swell from 2-6 feet. Heavy surf closes out. **Comment:** Typical beach surf, nothing exciting. Same surf can be found in Coronado without the walk.

Coronado Beach

An unpredictable beach break. Shape depends on contour of the sand bottom. Small (1-5 foot) peaky swells are best. Lined up swells usually close out. Medium-low tide. **Comment:** Few hazards . . . a safe spot when the surf is small.

Silver Strand State Park

A mile or so of unpredictable beach peaks. Break on most swells. Makeable from 1-5 feet medium tide. Closes out during heavy surf. **Comment:** Good swimming and bodysurfing during summer months . . . but **no** overnight camping.

Imperial Beach

Well-shaped beach peaks with fast right and left lines. Breaks on any swell from 2-6 feet. Medium-low tide. Shape is best during a clean west swell. **Note:** The popular spots include both sides of the pier and the two rock jetties at the foot of Palm Avenue.

SOUTHERN CALIFORNIA

TIJUANA SLOUGHS

A spooky, big-wave break. Lines peak on outer reefs and peel both left and right. Breaks summer and winter. Ridable from 2 feet up . . . never closes out. Big west swells are best. The following peaks are surfed.

Outer Peak

Big, gnarly, walls. Starts to work around 15 feet. Hairball takeoffs followed by a huge but makeable right line. Rarely (if ever) ridden . . . complete insanity.

Middle Peak

Takes over at 8 feet and will hold to 15. Peak explodes over a shallow reef- then quickly backs off as it peels right.

Inside Peak

Mild rights or fast hollow lefts. Starts cooking around 2 feet and closes out at 8. Lefts end in a pounding shorebreak.

Caution: Heavy rip currents, frequent sharks, blinding fogs and massive clean up sets . . . for some reason it's never crowded.

Note: The lefts are makeable from each peak. They're usually faster and better shaped. **But** . . . there is no return channel. If you're inside when a set rolls through - forget it and head for the beach.

The "middle peak" — TIJUANA SLOUGHS.

The "inside peak" — TIJUANA SLOUGHS.

Low tide lines at Imperial Beach.

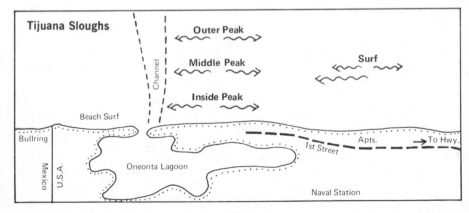

CORONADO BEACH. Banking off the bottom of a thick shoulder.

TIJUANA SLOUGHS — Perfect but dangerous lefts smoke off the reef at "middle peak".
See "notes" on page 172 for further explanation.

An evening glass settles over the ocean at SILVER STRAND STATE PARK.

Surf Spot Index

Credit

Research and Text — Bank Wright
California Maps — Sharyn M. Prentiss
Photography — Leroy Grannis
      — Peter Van Dyke
      — Jim Young
      — Dan Merkel
      — Kevin Egan
      — Bank Wright
      — International Surfing Magazine
Typesetting — Harry Theile Klein
Page Layout — Sharyn M. Prentiss
Cover Design — Rusty Kay
Printing — The Tivoli Printing Company, Los Angeles, California

Acknowledgements

I am sincerely grateful to the following persons:

Dr. and Mrs. Robert Scott, Mr. and Mrs. Alex Dias and Family, Mr. and Mrs. Bob Jensen, Dr. and Mrs. John H. Ball, Steve Mitchell, Jay Ball, Scott Wessling, Skip and Suzzane Miller, Jerry Grantham and wife, Austin, Patty and Gwendolyn, and the Waters Family.
Paul Brinkman, Larry, Sharyn and Benjamin Prentiss. Fred and Alice Hecklinger.

Without the help and encouragement of these people this book would not have been possible.

                ALOHA KE AKUA
                BANK WRIGHT

Dedication

This book is dedicated to:

  Mr. and Mrs. Allan B. Wright and all people who love and respect the oceans of the world.